The Pygmalion Project:
Love and Coercion Among the Types

The Pygmalion Project:
Love and Coercion Among the Types

Stephen Montgomery

 Prometheus Nemesis Book Company

Composition: Regina Books

Printing and Bindery: Book Crafters

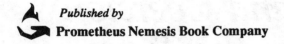

Published by
Prometheus Nemesis Book Company

First Edition

Printed in the United States of America

10   9   8   7   6   5   4   3   2   1

Library of Congress Card Catalog No:

ISBN: 0-9606954-5-1

Volume Two:

The Guardian

Acknowledgements

Thanks are due the following publishers for permission to reprint passages from the works cited:

Samuel French, Inc.: *A Doll House*, by Henrik Ibsen, trans. Rolfe Fjelde, copyright 1965.

Grove Press, Inc.: *The Norman Conquests*, by Alan Ayckbourn, copyright 1975.

Harcourt, Brace, Jovanovich, Inc.: *To the Lighthouse*, by Virginia Woolf, copyright 1927, renewed 1955 by Leonard Woolf.

Houghton, Mifflen Co.: *Pride and Prejudice*, by Jane Austen, ed. Mark Schorer, copyright 1956.

Little, Brown, & Co., Division of Time, Inc: *The African Queen*, by C.S. Forester, copyright 1935 by Cecil Scott Forester; copyright 1940 by Random House, Inc.; copyright renewed 1963 by Cecil Scott Forester; copyright renewed 1968 by Dorothy E. Forester; *A Handful of Dust*, copyright 1934 by Evelyn Waugh; copyright renewed 1962 by Evelyn Waugh.

New American Library: *Babbitt*, by Sinclair Lewis, copyright 1950; *Tess of the D'Urbervilles*, by Thomas Hardy.

Oxford University Press: *The School for Scandal*, by Richard Brinsley Sheridan, ed. C.J.L. Prince, copyright 1971.

Viking Penguin, Inc.: *Sons and Lovers*, by D.H. Lawrence, copyright 1913 by Thomas Seltzer, Inc.

Contents

Foreword

I'm delighted with this second volume in Stephen Montgomery's series on the Pygmalion Project. Dr. Montgomery gives us more of his fascinating character portraits, with more compelling insight into our lives and our marriages; but he also reminds us that novelists, playrights, and screen writers have a much keener eye (and ear) for mating games and tactics than the great majority of behavioral scientists up until the Haley-Erickson revolution.

Marriage, first of all, is perhaps the most important of all our human relationships, and certainly one of the most manipulative. As I have argued in *Please Understand Me*, and as Montgomery skillfully demonstrates in *The Pygmalion Project*, the marriage license is all too often taken as just that: the license to refashion our mate's character to be more like our own. I say *character* pointedly in order to distinguish, as I should in this context, between character and temperament. That is to say, we are born with our temperament, but we acquire our character progressively in life, as our temperament collides or converges, as the case may be, with our social environment. Temperament, since it is inborn, cannot be altered by any accidental or purposive interpersonal manipulation. But character can be, and more often than not *is,* altered by well-meaning albeit ill-advised spouses and parents. You see, character is what we *habitually do.* And we can get into the habit of doing the damnedest things! Especially if we are maneuvered or forced into double bind situations, which call forth our self-defensive tactics. Thus it is when we are cornered in our relationships that we unconsciously and involuntarily begin to play our unfriendly games, intending to make our spouse or parent rue the day he or she cornered us. And we all corner our loved ones and manipulate them in some degree, no matter how much we deny it, or wish to ascribe the tactical games to our spouse, parent, or offspring. All of us. No exceptions.

The second point raised by Dr. Montgomery's books is that writers of aesthetic fictions enjoy the enormous advantage of observing and describing human interactions in real-life situations, while the writers of *scientific* fictions (patient case studies and clinical research reports) have erred in confining themselves either to experimental or clinical situations, both of which yield only unusual behavior under unusual circumstances. Characters in novels and plays are not "real," of course, but they are based upon the close observation of real behavior in real people in the writer's real experience. And thus the "mirror" of fiction, as Montgomery calls it, comes much closer to observing human conduct in real human contexts than do the social scientists in their "controlled" and therefore dehumanized contexts.

The simple truth is that clinical and social psychology (even combined with sociology) have made very little progress during the 20th century in decoding human interaction. All were upstaged by a lonely communications scientist, Jay Haley, in cahoots with a lonely anthropologist, Gregory Bateson, and a lonely medic, Milton Erickson. These solitary outsiders broke the log jam in the late 50's and revealed the truth about human relationships—that they are at once dramatic scenarios and tactical games, apparently something aesthetic fiction writers as far back as Shakespeare have been intimately aware of.

Montgomery's literary case studies are particularly intriguing in this volume, for the Guardian's way in love and marriage is the role model in England and America, and any deviation from this traditional scenario is seen, by most of us at least, as unseemly and improper. The Guardian marital role, which came to its fullest flower during the long reign of Queen Victoria, rules us all to a certain extent, but the Guardians among us are devotedly and steadfastly Victorian. And there are so many of them—at least 45% in the population. They get married younger, raise more children, and stay married longer than the other types. Even when they divorce they quickly remarry, more often than not to the same personality type they parted from. Guardian married life is truly the standard against which all married life is measured in our culture, and—regardless of our type—Montgomery's illuminating portraits can make us more aware of the dramatic and tactical nature of our own relationships.

David Keirsey,
April, 1990

The Mirror
of Fiction

*It is not our purpose to become each other; it is to recognize
each other, to learn to see the other and honor him for what
he is.*

———Hermann Hesse[1]

In Greek legend, Pygmalion, a brilliant young sculptor from
Cyprus, was so disgusted (yet, strangely, so obsessed) with
women's imperfections that he resolved to carve a statue of
his ideal woman, embodying every feminine grace and
virtue. Determined to perfect in his art what he found so
flawed in flesh and blood, Pygmalion labored with all his
skill and devotion, shaping here, smoothing there, until he
had fashioned the most exquisite sculpture he could imagine. So exquisite indeed was his creation that Pygmalion
fell passionately in love with the figure, and could be seen
in his studio kissing its marble lips, fingering its marble
hands, dressing and grooming the statue as if caring for a
doll. Despite the work's perfection, however, Pygmalion

---

[1] Hermann Hesse, *Narcissus and Goldmund*, trans. Ursule Molinaro
(New York, 1968), p. 43.

was desperately unhappy, for the lifeless statue could not respond to his desires, the cold stone could not return the warmth of his love. He had set out to shape his idea of the perfect woman, but had succeeded only in creating his own frustration and despair.[2]

The premise of this book is that, in many of our closest relationships, we are ourselves Pygmalions. Not content with our loved ones' perfectly human differences, we set about to change them, to sculpt them into our conception of what they should be. At first we are attracted by their separate temperaments, intrigued by creatures distinct from ourselves; but the more intimate we grow (and the more we see our loved ones as reflections of ourselves), the more we come to see these differences as imperfections—and the more we assume the responsibility for correcting them. We snipe and criticize, brow-beat and bully, we sculpt with guilt and with flattery, with logic and with tears—whatever strategies are most natural to us. Instead of appreciating and nurturing our loved ones' different ways of living, we selfishly try to perfect them into copies of ourselves or our ideals. Not that we do this ceaselessly, nor always maliciously, but all too often, almost without thinking, we fall into this pattern of coercive behavior.

And like Pygmalion, we are inevitably frustrated, for our well-intentioned efforts to make people over only bring us disappointment and conflict. Our loved ones do not—cannot—comply meekly with our coercions, and even if

---

[2] Summarized from Edith Hamilton's *Mythology* (Mentor ed.), pp. 108-111.

they did we would be taking from them what surely attracted us in the first place, their integrity, their distinct breath of life. Our Pygmalion projects must fail: either our loved ones fight back, and our most intimate relationships become battlegrounds, or our loved ones give in to us, and become as lifeless as Pygmalion's statue. In this paradoxical game, we lose even if we win.

Of course, in the legend, Venus took pity on Pygmalion and brought his statue to life, and he and "Galatea," as he named her, blushed, embraced, and married with the goddess's blessing. The rest of us, however, cannot rely on such miraculous intervention. We must indeed take responsibility for our own relationships, but instead of resorting to coercion, we must try to abandon our Pygmalion projects, by learning, if we can, to understand and to honor our fundamental differences in temperament. If we can respect the right of our loved ones to be different from ourselves—to be perfect in their own ways—then we can begin to bring the beauty of our own relationships alive.

The argument of my books is not entirely new. I take my main title, in fact, from David Keirsey and Marilyn Bates's *Please Understand Me: Character and Temperament Types,* and throughout these pages I am indebted to their wonderfully perceptive analysis of human behavior and relationship styles. However, the nature of my evidence— literary characters—*is* unusual, and needs perhaps a few words of explanation. For if Pygmalion's attempt to shape human life into art was misguided, then the opposite impulse, to see in art the shape of human life, is the very basis of my discussions.

I make at the outset one I hope not too obvious assumption: that the skillful novelist (playwright, poet) and the skillful temperament psychologist are both, of necessity, skillful people-watchers. The cornerstone of realistic fiction has always been the story-teller's astute observation of human behavior. We marvel at how "lifelike" are his characters or how "true-to-life" are their experiences. The so-called "Romantic" and "Symbolist" writers may have loftier visions, but they base their fictions nonetheless on authentic human types before they transcend to their ideal worlds or retreat into their private fantasies. Even such clearly unrealistic forms of fiction as myth and caricature build upon a sharp-eyed perception of human characteristics. Thus the Greek epic heroes, as well as the gods, are plagued with all our human foibles, and Charles Dickens's most grotesque characters embody our most familiar human traits. As one literary critic has put it:

> Literature portrays almost every conceivable human action, thought, attitude, emotion, situation, or problem. In one way or another people are basic to the literary imagination, even in its most fanciful flights.[3]

Certainly fictional characters are not real people, and to insist on their reality may close us off from an author's

---

[3] B. Bernard Cohen, *Writing About Literature* (Glenview, Illinois, 1973), p. 37.

distinctive view of the world. Still, when a story catches, as Henry James described it, "the very note and trick, the strange irregular rhythm" of human behavior, we know that we are "touching truth" and breathing the "air of reality."[4] In other words, when a story lives for us and catches us up in its artifice, most often it is because we see ourselves and our predicaments in its pages, and such a personal recognition can delight us—or disturb us profoundly—with its insight. Knowing this, Hamlet instructed a troup of actors to catch his uncle's conscience with a play—and defined the power of fiction to make us perceive ourselves more clearly:

> the purpose of playing... was and is, to hold, as 'twere, the mirror up to nature.[5]

In much the same way, the writing of the more perceptive temperament psychologists also unnerves us with this rush of recognition. To read David Keirsey's sixteen character portraits in *Please Understand Me* is to look in a mirror indeed. When I began to edit *Please Understand Me*, I remember browsing ahead in the manuscript and being a little shaken by the air of truth in my own portrait, the "NF" Author, as Keirsey called it then. I felt quite found out at the time, almost as if some novelist or playwright had sketched me in his working notebook. (A decade of reports from *Please Understand Me* readers of all types suggests

---

[4] Henry James, "The Art of Fiction" in *Partial Portraits* (Ann Arbor, 1970), pp. 398, 390.

[5] William Shakespeare, *Hamlet*, III, ii, 19-20.

such unmasking is frequently the case.) I found the other portraits nearly as fascinating (no one is quite as fascinating as oneself), and as I worked on the manuscript I realized that Keirsey's word portraits of Isabel Myers's four-letter designations (the Inspector for Myers's "ISTJ," the Performer for the "ESFP," and so on) were offering me an extraordinary instrument: a flexible and surprisingly accurate vocabulary for discussing the welter of human personality.

As with all experience of a new vocabulary, I began to see the world around me with new clarity and in new detail, and very soon my family, my students, my colleagues, friends and foes alike, found their way into the categories of personality I was internalizing. Not that they were reduced from complex, unique individuals, but the broader lines of their attitudes and imperatives came into focus. And in my work—reading and teaching literature—I made a two-fold discovery. Not only could I comprehend literary characters with more insight, but I began to see that throughout history the great novelists and playwrights had been bringing to life the same gallery of real life characters that Keirsey was describing in *Please Understand Me*, and in his more recent book, *Portraits of Temperament*. The impulsive "SP" Artisans and the spiritual "NF" Idealists, the logical "NT" Rationals and the dutiful "SJ" Guardians, all kinds and combinations of these characters lived in the pages of Chaucer, Shakespeare, Jane Austen, Dickens, D.H. Lawrence, Hemingway, and many, many more.

To be sure, literary characters give themselves, in most cases, to this sort of category, providing the most amazing illustrations of Keirsey's type portraits. After all, as the critic Robert Scholes has argued, writers create their characters from two impulses: "the impulse to individualize and the impulse to typify."[6] Authors (particularly "NF" Idealist authors) cherish the mystery of the individual and bristle at the idea of putting unique human beings into boxes; but the best of them also admit that their characters typify larger categories of humanity. Indeed, much of the interest (and the charm) of fiction lies in its power to be discriminating and representative at the same time. Thus Henry James cautions us that "Humanity is immense, and reality has a myriad forms,"[7] but he also understands that "Art is essentially selection...whose main care is to be typical."[8] Professional literary critics have long endeavored to unravel characters' individual complexities with the help of psychological analysis; temperament theory can now provide us with a finer language (a finer "vocabulary" as I have called it) for recognizing the broader patterns of human behavior, first in the characters and then in ourselves.

My hope in these books, then, is to marry these two characterologies into an informative and I hope entertaining look at the different ways people go about their closest relationships. I want to demonstrate that, by seeing literary

---

6 Robert Scholes, *Elements of Literature* (New York, 1978), p. 109.
7 Henry James, "The Art of Fiction" in *Partial Portraits*, pp. 387-8.
8 Henry James, "The Art of Fiction" in *Partial Portraits*, p. 398.

characters as discerning portraits of human character *styles* (Jay Gatsby as a Promoter Artisan, say, or Hamlet as an "NF" Idealist), we can learn a good deal about our own interpersonal games and strategies from literature—and perhaps discover a new interest in literature in the process. In other words, by regarding the lives of literary characters as virtual case studies of the Keirseyan Types, we can, in the mirror of these fictions, better perceive ourselves and our own Pygmalion projects. Which returns me to the topic of my books, potentially the most coercive relationship of all: Love.

Approaching temperament styles through literature in one way broadens the field of research—all of those stories, all of those characters—but it also narrows the focus to those subjects that literature most eloquently addresses. And certainly the subject upon which literature lavishes most attention and reveals most insight is, by far, love. Love, courtship, passion, marriage, this "constant sensitiveness of characters for each other," as E.M. Forster described it, "this constant awareness, this endless readjustment, this ceaseless hunger"[9]—love in all its forms and complications fascinates the literary imagination, and provides a wealth of detail for the reader with an eye for character types. Indeed, the strategies of love so tirelessly pursued in novels and plays amply illustrate Keirsey's portraits of the Artisan, Guardian, Rational, and Idealist mating styles, as well as largely support his theory of the Pygmalion project. For

---

9 E.M. Forster, *Aspects of the Novel* (Harvest ed., 1954), pp. 54-5.

better or for worse, we do seem irresistibly attracted to other types, and we do attempt—and almost invariably with unfortunate consequences—to reshape our loved ones in our own image. This too is the abundant evidence of literature.

Literature and temperament theory thus combined offer us more than either fictitious characters or oversimplified categories. Broadly defined by the temperament psychologist and richly detailed by the novelist or playwright, these are *our* relationships, depicting our attractions and regrets, our dreams and strategies, our coercions and compromises. If we will look carefully into the mirror of fiction, we can come to understand ourselves more clearly, and perhaps recognize the Pygmalion in us all.

But first, to those of you unfamiliar with temperament theory, or who have forgotten exactly what all the capital letters ("SP," "NT," etc.) and all the talk about "temperaments" and "types" is about, I want to offer the following diagnostic summary, newly formulated by David Keirsey, and printed with his permission. You might first want to find the columns, and thus the temperament styles, that best describe you and your loved ones, though certainly a summary knowledge of the four basic styles will help you with my character descriptions in this volume. Remember that the following table is a short-hand classifier; for a more complete personality survey, take Keirsey's Temperament

Sorter questionnaire in *Please Understand Me* (reproduced in the Appendix at the back of this book). Remember also that all of us have *all* of these characteristics, and surely many more, and that our temperament is merely a characteristic dominance in our behavior of one style over the others.

The two following pages: Keirsey's Brief Character Sorter, reproduced by permission of Dr. David Keirsey.

KEIRSEY'S BRIEF CHARACTER SORTER

First read down the four lettered columns to get a quick impression of which one describes you best. Then read each row and circle one of the four words that fits you better than the others. Skip rows that are hard to decide. When finished add the number of words in each column and place the number in the box at the bottom of each column. If your quick impression and your word choices point to one of the columns, you have identified your personality type. If they do not, you might ask your family and friends which applies to you best.

	A	B	C	D
I'm better at	refashioning	stabilizing	differentiating	integrating
I prefer	crafting	safeguarding	reasoning	idealizing
I like feeling	excited	concerned	calm	inspired
I look for	happenings	security	problems	meanings
I'm better at	expediting	monitoring	entailing	guiding
I like being	a winner	accountable	competent	authentic
I often crave	stimulation	ownership	achievement	caring
I tend to be	funloving	stoical	empirical	romantic
I try to be	practical	traditional	pragmatic	ethical
I'm better at	improvising	providing	engineering	teaching
I explain with	pictures	specifics	categories	attributions
I like to appear	cool	staunch	intelligent	special
I'm sometimes	cynical	fatalistic	nihilistic	mystical
I'm better at	promoting	supervising	marshalling	teaching
I'd like to be	nervy	charitable	autonomous	benevolent
I'd rather be	a virtuoso	a dignitary	a genius	a sage
I'm better at	toolworking	inspecting	sequencing	counseling
I think about	what is	what was	what may be	what can be
I'm sometimes	optimistic	pessimistic	skeptical	credulous
I'm better at	performing	supplying	inventing	investigating
I'm confident if	strong	acceptable	strongwilled	empathic
I often think of	tactics	supplies	strategies	diplomacy
I speak of	what works	particulars	principles	similarities
I put my trust in	luck	authority	evidence	conscience
I think about	the here & now	in's & out's	intersections	paths of life
I'm sometimes	reckless	depressed	preoccupied	estranged
I'm better at	composing	protecting	architecting	conciliating

total A _____   total B _____   total C _____   total D _____

Artisan Type   Guardian Type   Rational Type   Idealist Type

KEIRSEY'S BRIEF CHARACTER SORTER

First read down the four lettered columns to get a quick impression of which one describes you best. Then read each row and circle one of the four words that fits you better than the others. Skip rows that are hard to decide. When finished add the number of words in each column and place the number in the box at the bottom of each column. If your quick impression and your word choices point to one of the columns, you have identified your personality type. If they do not, you might ask your family and friends which applies to you best.

	A	B	C	D
I'm better at	refashioning	stabilizing	differentiating	integrating
I prefer	crafting	safeguarding	reasoning	idealizing
I like feeling	excited	concerned	calm	inspired
I look for	happenings	security	problems	meanings
I'm better at	expediting	monitoring	entailing	guiding
I like being	a winner	accountable	competent	authentic
I often crave	stimulation	ownership	achievement	caring
I tend to be	funloving	stoical	empirical	romantic
I try to be	practical	traditional	pragmatic	ethical
I'm better at	improvising	providing	engineering	teaching
I explain with	pictures	specifics	categories	attributions
I like to appear	cool	staunch	intelligent	special
I'm sometimes	cynical	fatalistic	nihilistic	mystical
I'm better at	promoting	supervising	marshalling	teaching
I'd like to be	nervy	charitable	autonomous	benevolent
I'd rather be	a virtuoso	a dignitary	a genius	a sage
I'm better at	toolworking	inspecting	sequencing	counseling
I think about	what is	what was	what may be	what can be
I'm sometimes	optimistic	pessimistic	skeptical	credulous
I'm better at	performing	supplying	inventing	investigating
I'm confident if	strong	acceptable	strongwilled	empathic
I often think of	tactics	supplies	strategies	diplomacy
I speak of	what works	particulars	principles	similarities
I put my trust in	luck	authority	evidence	conscience
I think about	the here & now	in's & out's	intersections	paths of life
I'm sometimes	reckless	depressed	preoccupied	estranged
I'm better at	composing	protecting	architecting	conciliating

total A ___	total B ___	total C ___	total D ___
Artisan Type	Guardian Type	Rational Type	Idealist Type

Chapter 1

The Rites of Autumn

Where are the songs of Spring? Ay, where are they?
Think not of them, thou hast thy music too.

——John Keats[1]

The ancient Greeks worshipped two great gods of the earth, or of earthly, *physical* existence. One was a relative upstart, Dionysus, the god of fertility and the vine, and his festival—held in the spring of the year—welcomed the land's release from the bitter grip of winter. But a much older and more venerated earth deity was Demeter, the goddess of grain and the harvest, and though she shared dominion with Dionysus over nature's abundance, her worship was as different from his as corn is from wine.

First of all, Dionysus was celebrated in the spring, the season of rebirth and procreation, while Demeter's festival

---

[1] John Keats, "To Autumn," ll. 23-24.

was held in the fall, the season, as Keats put it, of "soft-dying day," consecrating the harvest as the year turned toward the long, barren months of winter. Secondly, Dionysus had no temple but the wild woodlands and no rituals other than orgiastic revels,[2] whereas Demeter's altar was simply prepared in the harvest fields and on the threshing room floor, and her temple at Eleusis was the seat of the Eleusinian Mysteries, solemn ceremonies which Cicero later credited with civilizing the classical world: "they have made us pass," he believed, "from the condition of savages to true humanity." Furthermore, Dionysus' worship drew its ecstasy from the free flow of wine, while Demeter's proceeded calmly and silently with a cup of barley-water and the humble act of breaking bread. And finally, if Dionysus lifted his revelers to joyous release in his orgies, then Demeter burdened her disciples with sorrow and apprehension in her simple rituals, asking them to mourn each winter for the loss of her beloved daughter, Persephone, when the dark lord of the underworld carried Persephone away to his deathly kingdom and held her hostage until spring's return.[3]

During the autumn months, then, Demeter reigned over the domesticated and responsible side of Greek physical life. She was the goddess of duty and useful work, of protection

---

[2] Over the centuries, the frenzy and blood sacrifice of these revels were tamed into the terror and beauty of Greek drama, presented each spring in the Fesitval of Dionysus.

[3] Summarized from Edith Hamilton's *Mythology* (Mentor ed.), pp. 47-54.

and husbandry and sober procedure, of the blessed security of a safe harvest, but also of the grave, relentless approach of winter's hardships. And thus, if Dionysus epitomized the exuberant, springtime character of the Artisans in *The Pygmalion Project*, *Volume One*, then Demeter stands quite properly in this second volume for the more cautious and sensible temperament David Keirsey names the Guardians.

Indeed, the Guardians ("SJ's" in Myers's terminology) consider the first rule of life to be duty, and they take on obligations and responsibilities with a seriousness of purpose that at times clouds their very features. The Guardian is Oscar Wilde's Mr. Ernest Worthing, whose earnest concern for his ward worries the young girl about his health. "Sometimes he is so serious," she confesses, "that I think he cannot be quite well," though her governess quickly reassures her:

> Your guardian enjoys the best of health, and his gravity of demeanour is especially to be commended....I know of no one who has a higher sense of duty and responsibility.[4]

Guardians believe in being useful, in caring for others, in cooperating and doing their part, and they can easily find themselves overburdened with added responsibilities, and quite often feel unappreciated for their efforts. The Guardian is J.R.R. Tolkein's hospitable little hobbit, Bilbo Baggins, who finds himself cleaning up after a pack of

---

[4] Oscar Wilde, *The Importance of Being Earnest* (Avon ed., 1965), p. 57.

adventurous but thoroughly ungrateful dwarves, Artisans every one of them:

> By the time he had got all the bottles and dishes and knives
> and forks and glasses and plates and spoons and things piled
> up on big trays, he was getting very hot, and red in the face,
> and annoyed.
> "Confusticate and bebother these dwarves!" he said aloud.
> "Why don't they come and lend a hand?"[5]

Even more than doing their duty, Guardians care about doing things in the right way, and this means by respecting traditions and authorities, and by obeying rules and accepted procedures. The Guardian is Shakespeare's Malvolio (his name literally means "ill wind"), who chastises a group of noisy Artisan revellers:

> My Masters, are you mad? or what are you? Have you no wit,
> manners, nor honesty?... Is there no respect of place, persons,
> nor time in you?[6]

"Person, place, and time" are particularly dear to the Guardians, and they pay their respects by conscientiously maintaining time-honored places and personal possessions. The Guardian is Anton Chekov's Madame Ranevsky, who cherishes the past and weeps at the thought of selling off her family's prized cherry orchard to pay their debts:

> I was born here, you know, my father and mother lived here,
> my grandfather lived here, I love this house. I can't conceive

---

5 J.R.R. Tolkein, *The Hobbit* (Ballantine ed., 1965), p. 24.
6 William Shakespeare, *Twelfth Night*, II,iii,87-93.

of life without the cherry orchard, and if it really must be sold, then sell me with the orchard.[7]

Wedded in this way to tradition, Guardians feel most at home in long-established hierarchies, and often admire the power and prestige of the aristocracy. Thus Firs, the old valet in *The Cherry Orchard*, refused his freedom when the serfs were emancipated ("the peasants knew their place," he grumbles, "and the masters knew theirs"), and sees the old ways as the only ways:

> The old master, the grandfather, used to give sealing-wax for all complaints. I have been taking sealing-wax for twenty years or more. Perhaps that's what's kept me alive.[8]

Guardians also try to govern their lives by truisms and homilies, hoping to instruct their behavior with the conventional lessons of the past. The Guardian is Shakespeare's garrulous old minister, Polonious, who cautions his son Laertes against the Dionysian lures of life in France with a catalogue of truly Guardian precepts:

> Give thy thoughts no tongue,
> Nor any unproportioned thought his act.
> Be thou familiar, but by no means vulgar...
> Costly thy habit as thy purse can buy,
> But not expressed in fancy; rich, not gaudy...
> Neither a borrower nor a lender be,
> For loan oft loses both itself and friend,
> And borrowing dulleth the edge of husbandry.[9]

---

[7] Anton Chekov, *The Cherry Orchard*, in *Four Great Plays by Chekov*, trans. Constance Garnett (Bantam ed., 1968), pp. 98-99.

[8] Anton Chekov, *The Cherry Orchard*, in *Four Great Plays by Chekov*, trans. Constance Garnett (Bantam ed., 1968), p. 101.

[9] William Shakespeare, *Hamlet*, I,iii,58-77.

In times of uncertainty, Guardians prefer to go by the book, with full assurance that their actions are not whimsical or improvised, but follow approved, authorized, time-tested procedures. The Guardian is Joseph Conrad's imperturbable Captain MacWhirr, whose literal mind cannot quite understand his first mate's jitters at sailing under a new and ominous-looking Siamese flag:

> "Well, it looks queer to me," burst out Jukes, greatly exasperated, and flung off the bridge.
> Captain MacWhirr was amazed at these manners. After a while he stepped quietly into the chartroom and opened his International Signal Codebook at the plate where the flags of all the nations are correctly figured... and when he came to Siam he contemplated with great attention the red field and the white elephant. Nothing could be more simple. "There's nothing amiss with that flag....Length twice the breadth and the elephant exactly in the middle."[10]

Because they observe their standards of conduct so religiously, Guardians can grow impatient with the world's—particularly the Artisan world's—lack of discipline and general disrespect for civilized manners and morals. The Guardian is John Fowles's Mrs. Poultney, who oversees her Victorian household with antiseptic propriety:

> Mrs. Poultney had two obsessions: One was Dirt... and the other was Immorality. In neither field did anything untoward escape her eagle eye.[11]

---

10 Joseph Conrad, *Typhoon* in *Three Great Tales* (Vintage ed., 1971), p. 143.
11 John Fowles, *The French Lieutenant's Woman* (Signet ed., 1970), p. 22.

The Guardian is also the accountant in Conrad's *Heart of Darkness*, who, surrounded by the "great demoralization" of the African jungle, stubbornly and admirably sits on his high stool and strives to keep the Company's books in order. "It is extremely difficult to guard against clerical errors in this climate," he complains, gazing at the crush of natives in the station-yard; "when one has got to make correct entries, one comes to hate those savages."[12] And the Guardian is Chaucer's Reeve (an estate steward), whose scrupulous management makes the most of Demeter's blessings:

> He kept his bins and garners very trim;
> No auditor could gain a point on him.
> And he could judge by watching drought and rain
> The yield he might expect from seed and grain.[13]

This constant watchfulness—a kind of in-born vigilance against things being out of place or going wrong—makes the Guardians the trustworthy custodians of our civilization, and without them we would likely have succumbed to Dionysian chaos by now. But such conscientious safekeeping can darken the Guardian's attitude as surely as it clouds his demeanor. Guardians at times take on an air of gloom and doom as they view the world's frivolous ways. The Guardian is Lane, the manservant in *The Importance of Being Earnest*, who does his best to dampen a love-struck Artisan's incorrigible optimism:

---

[12] Joseph Conrad, *Heart of Darkness* (Norton Critical ed., 1971), p. 19.
[13] Geoffrey Chaucer, *The Canterbury Tales*, trans. Nevill Coghill (Penguin ed.), p. 37.

ALGERNON. I hope tomorrow will be a fine day, Lane.
LANE. It never is, sir
ALGERNON. Lane, you're a perfect pessimist.
LANE. I do my best to give satisfaction, sir.[14]

And the Guardian is Kurt Vonnegut's Ransom K. Fern, a one-time I.R.S. agent and now corporate C.E.O., whose dour philosophy of life sums up the Guardian's characteristically depressive[15] outlook:

> ...you see things really couldn't be much worse. When you get right down to it, everybody's having a perfectly lousy time of it, and I mean everybody. And the hell of it is, nothing seems to help much.[16]

Clearly, the Guardians are well-represented in fiction, and play important roles in virtually every category of literature. They are the hero in a good number of stories, such as the "faithfull true" but also "solemn sad" Redcrosse Knight in Edmund Spenser's *The Fairie Queene,* or Daniel Defoe's industrious castaway, Robinson Crusoe, or Leopold Bloom, James Joyce's modern incarnation of the epic hero in *Ulysses,* or Tevye the milkman in *Fiddler on the Roof,* who sings of "Tradition" throughout the play. But far more often they are minor characters who frame the action or serve the heroes, characters such as Mr. Lockwood and Nelly Dean, Emily Brontë's convention-bound narrators in *Wuthering*

---

14 Oscar Wilde, *The Importance of Being Earnest,* (Avon ed., 1965), p. 55.
15 David Keirsey, *Portraits of Temperament,* pp. 51, 61-62.
16 Kurt Vonnegut, *The Sirens of Titan* (Delta ed., 1959), p. 69.

Heights, or Conan Doyle's sensible, dependable Dr. Watson, or good Mrs. Bread (a name Demeter would approve) in Henry James's *The American,* or even such a fastidious character as T.S. Eliot's J. Alfred Prufrock, who confesses,

> No! I am not Prince Hamlet, nor was meant to be;
> Am an attendant lord, one that will do
> To swell a progress, start a scene or two,
> Advise the prince; no doubt, an easy tool,
> Deferential, glad to be of use,
> Politic, cautious, and meticulous.[17]

Indeed, the Guardians are most commonly cast as the "meticulous" keepers of the status quo, the conventional characters against whom the Artisans, Rationals, and Idealists struggle to find their freedom. Guardians are typically parental figures, such as Tom Sawyer's Aunt Polly, Balzac's Pére Goriot, Clarence Day in *Life with Father,* or Ma Joad in John Steinbeck's *The Grapes of Wrath.* They are military officers, such as Mister Claggert in Melville's *Billy Budd,* Captain Queeg in Herman Wouk's *The Caine Mutiny*—or caricatures such as Frank Barnes in *M*A*S*H,* or Lieutenant Sheisskopf in Joseph Heller's *Catch 22.* Often they are clergymen, the amiable Mr. Harding in Anthony Trollope's *The Warden,* for instance, or Edward Casaubon in George Eliot's *Middlemarch.* Or they are medical authorities, such as Big Nurse Ratched in Ken Kesey's *One Flew over the Cuckoo's Nest,* or the caustic Dr. Sloper in James's *Washington Square.*

---

[17] T.S. Eliot, "The Love Song of J. Alfred Prufrock," ll. 114-119.

Guardians can be businessmen such as William Dean Howells's Silas Lapham, or Thornton Wilder's Horace Van der Gelder in *The Matchmaker* (filmed as *Hello Dolly*). They can be lawyers such as Ivan Ilych in Tolstoy's *The Death of Ivan Ilych*, or Bertie Reid, the Scottish barrister in D.H. Lawrence's haunting short story, "The Blind Man." Or they can be schoolmasters such as Dickens's heartless Thomas Gradgrind in *Hard Times*, or James Hilton's long-faithful Mr. Chips. To be sure, Guardians can be cold, embittered figures in literature, such as Shakespeare's Shylock, or Jason Compson in Faulkner's *The Sound and the Fury,* or Beth Jarrett, the emotionally frozen mother in Judith Guest's novel, *Ordinary People.* But just as often they are kind-hearted and sociable characters, Dickens's Aunt Betsey Trotwood in *David Copperfield*, for example, or Macon Leary in Anne Tyler's *The Accidental Tourist*— or the Muppets' frazzled but indefatigable manager, Kermit the Frog.

The focus of these volumes, however, is on the coercive behavior of the four temperaments as lovers and marriage partners—their characteristic styles of Pygmalion projects—and here the evidence of literature suggests that the Guardians are particularly devoted sculptors. With their innate belief in duty and procedure, their highly disciplined sense of "shoulds and shouldn'ts," and their essentially civilizing outlook on life, Guardians seem to emerge from the womb already concerned about shaping up a negligent world. And when married to an iconoclastic Rational, say, or to a soul-searching Idealist, or particularly to an impulsive Artisan, any self-respecting Guardian sees his or her duty quite clearly. This is not to say that, in real life, all Guardians are single-minded Pygmalions, or that all Guardian marriages are grimly manipulative. But it does appear that the Guardians' parental disposition, especially when compared to the Artisans' childlike live-and-let-live attitude, seems naturally turned toward interpersonal coercion. Guardians care deeply that their loved ones, of whatever age, grow up and start acting respectfully, or sensibly, or responsibly, as the case may be, and in their intimate relationships at least, they are not shy about communicating their expectations.

David Keirsey sees significant differences among the Guardians, of course, as the following geneoalogy summarizes:

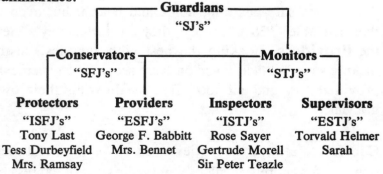

	Guardians "SJ's"		
Conservators "SFJ's"		Monitors "STJ's"	
Protectors	**Providers**	**Inspectors**	**Supervisors**
"ISFJ's"	"ESFJ's"	"ISTJ's"	"ESTJ's"
Tony Last	George F. Babbitt	Rose Sayer	Torvald Helmer
Tess Durbeyfield	Mrs. Bennet	Gertrude Morell	Sarah
Mrs. Ramsay		Sir Peter Teazle	

In his *Portraits of Temperament*, Keirsey divides the Guardian temperament into two major styles, the **Conservators** (Myers's "SFJ's") and the **Monitors** (Myers's "STJ's"), and this initial distinction suggests a good deal about their approach to interpersonal manipulation.

In general, the Conservators are less "role-directive"[18] than the Monitors, less comfortable confronting their loved ones with orders to straighten up and fly right. The Conservators are perhaps the nicest of all the personality styles, naturally cooperative in their relationships, even deferential at times, more interested in being reliable and considerate than in voicing their criticisms (think of Edith Bunker in *All In the Family*, or Charlie Brown in *Peanuts*). To the Conservators, selfishness is a cardinal sin, and making pointed demands on their loved ones is far too arrogant and self-serving for their taste. Much like the industrious squirrel, Conservators are instinctive nest-keepers, and perhaps their greatest fear is of doing anything that might scatter the nest or break apart the family unit. In their private ("ISFJ") mode, Keirsey calls them the **Protectors** to capture their quiet devotion to safe-guarding home and hearth; but even in their sociable ("ESFJ") mode, they are in Keirsey's view the **Providers**, stocking the nest with supplies, busily making sure that their loved ones are secure and generously provided for, and all too often swallowing their own grievances.

Conservators *have* their grievances, to be sure, and they don't suffer entirely in silence, but their style of expressing their displeasure is relatively oblique. Rather than complaining openly to their loved ones, Conservators may

---

[18] David Keirsey, *Portraits of Temperament*, p. 55.

let themselves appear slighted and hurt, or over-burdened and helpless, or they may even show themselves as suffering from anxiety or physical illness, attempting to elicit with subtle varieties of guilt-mongering ("no, no, I'm all right") the nurturing and appreciation they expect from their loved ones. Again, not all Conservators resort to such tactics, and not all the time, but in stressful relationships they seem so inclined.

The Monitors, on the other hand, often dispense with such indirection; if Charlie Brown is a Conservator Guardian, then Lucy is clearly a Monitor. Keirsey considers the Monitors as "role-directive" in their relationships,[19] which means that they are comfortable giving orders, believe it is their *duty* to shape up their loved ones, and even assume that their loved ones are grateful for being called on the errors of their ways. Monitors are often just as sociable in their relationships as Conservators, and just as disapproving of selfishness, but their concern for accepted standards of behavior is more tough-minded (more Archie Bunker's style than Edith's), and their need to make others toe the mark is more rigorous. If the Conservators are squirrels, then the Monitors are more like beavers, not simply building and stocking their lodges, but also standing stubborn guard on their ponds afterward, ready to drum out a warning if they spot anything amiss. Indeed, in their private ("ISTJ") mode, Keirsey calls them the **Inspectors**, the diligent, sharp-eyed examiners who carefully note their

---

[19] David Keirsey, *Portraits of Temperament*, p. 44.

loved ones' errors and deficiencies, while in their gregarious ("ESTJ") mode they are the **Supervisors**, the forthright enforcers of an institution's—or a relationship's—rules and rituals.

In hurtful relationships, however, when direct confrontation fails to shape the partner satisfactorily, Monitors may turn to similar interpersonal game tactics as the Conservators, though again with a harder edge. Monitors might actually accuse their loved ones of neglect, or complain of unfair and debilitating responsibilities ("must I do everything myself?"), or even resort to chronic exhaustion or hypochondriacal illness to extort the compliance they feel entitled to. If Conservators are master manipulators of the guilty conscience, then Monitors in their harshest Pygmalion projects are more likely to wear away at their loved ones with nagging criticism.

Guardians, with these compelling needs to belong and to serve, to nest and to nurture, are perhaps the most marriage-minded of all the temperaments, making loyal and sometimes long-suffering mates to the Rationals and the Idealists, and particularly to the Artisans. As I explained in *The Pygmalion Project, Volume One*, Artisans and Guardians seem to have a special affinity for one another, as if drawn together—Dionysus and Demeter—by a curious mutual attraction. And in most cases these "grasshopper and ant" marriages complement each other quite well, one spreading the seed and the other carefully managing the harvest. For Guardians, the impetuous Artisan is both a "child" to take care of and, at times, a wonderful diversion from their shoulder-to-the-wheel existence. For Artisans, on the other hand, the ever-responsibile Guardian is both a stable anchor for their foot-loose way of life and an "adult" they can enjoy surprising and loosening up with their spontaneity. Indeed, the evidence of literature suggests that these two temperaments, on the surface so incompatible, seem somehow to find each other with amazing regularity, from Petruchio and Katerina in Shakespeare's *The Taming of the Shrew* to Ralph and Alice Kramden in Jackie Gleason's *The Honeymooners*, from Tom and Sophy in Fielding's *Tom Jones* to Oscar and Felix in Neil Simon's *The Odd Couple*, from Robin Hood and Maid Marian to Lady and the Tramp.[20]

But literature also observes the inherent conflicts in the Guardian-Artisan marriage, and the novels and plays I take up in this volume examine when necessary these darker interactions. In the first place, the Guardian (and most often the female Guardian) can become slavishly devoted to her

---

20 Dan Kiley cites another fictional couple, Jame M. Barrie's Wendy and Peter Pan, as a prototype of a troubled Guardian-Artisan relationship. See Kiley's *The Wendy Dilemma* and *The Peter Pan Syndrome*. Kiley describes the futility of Wendy's Guardian Pygmalion project quite accurately, though his premise that Peter Pan (the childlike Artisan man) suffers from arrested development and secretly longs to grow up and "discover himself" is, it seems to me, an unfortunate misreading of both human personality and of Barrie's play. Being an Artisan is not a "ghastly affliction," as Kiley suggests, but a valuable way of life in its own right, and Barrie's Peter Pan is quite content to stay in his carefree, timeless world of Never-Never Land.

Artisan mate, addicted in some tortured way to saving her wayward lover, even at the cost of her own self-esteem. Her obsession with "re-forming" the Artisan by loving him into a more conscientious way of life can become a tragic debasement of her love, and she might suffer years of psychological and physical abuse before she gives up her hopeless Pygmalion project.[21] At the other extreme, when Guardians—male or female—become too domineering in their relationships, their strictness can turn to rigidity, their sobriety can turn to austerity, and their dutiful criticism can turn to scathing admonition. And what is for most Guardians an on-going, rather tolerant Pygmalion project (just a few reminders, "for your own good"[22]) can become a relentless effort to scold their childlike spouse into behaving sensibly, responsibly—like a Guardian—and almost invariably humiliating the Artisan into either abandoning the relationship or fighting back with destructive behavior.

Still, in all fairness, most Guardian Pygmalion projects are good-natured and well-intentioned. Guardians take their family responsibilities seriously, just as they take *all* responsibilities seriously, and they regard their interpersonal coercion as a necessary and a worthy, even a loving, attempt to make their loved ones into better human beings.

---

21 See Robin Norwood's *Women Who Love Too Much*, a perceptive study of what appears to be largely a Guardian female-Artisan male pattern of interpersonal abuse.

22 See Alice Miller's *For Your Own Good*, as well as her *Thou Shalt Not Be Aware* and *The Drama of the Gifted Child*, three brilliant—and chilling—books on the pernicious effects of traditional authoritarian (i.e. Guardian) parenting.

Unfortunately, literature all too often disparages even this relatively harmless Guardian intervention as being meddling and repressive, because novelists and playwrights tend to champion the romantic ideas of individual freedom, sexual liberation, and social revolution. And thus the Guardians' humble creed of following the rules, of nourishing traditions, of respecting order—and of fostering these beliefs in their loved ones—only occasionally receives in literature the fair treatment it deserves.

However, despite this wide-spread prejudice in literature against the Guardians, a good many novelists and playwrights recognize the simple truth that the loyal, reliable Guardians are the rock-solid foundation of all our civilized institutions, including marriage, and the authors I have chosen for this volume offer valuable and largely sympathetic insight into the Guardians' uniquely custodial style of loving.

Chapter 2

The
Protector

HANNAH (Softly) Look, can I help you? If you're suffering over something, will you share it with me?

——Woody Allen[1]

Of the four types of Guardians, the Protectors (Myers's "ISFJ's") appear the least coercive in their love relationships. Protectors, as their name implies, concern themselves far more with safeguarding their established relationships than with manipulating interpersonal change, and thus they make exceptionally loyal and dependable mates, supportive, comforting, and remarkably unassuming. Of course, quiet guardianship can itself become a subtle means of coercion. Miss Bartlett, the Protector chaperon in E.M. Forster's *A Room with a View*, for example, sees it as her duty to screen her cousin Lucy from the possible dangers of an Italian tour, and on their first night in

---

[1] Woody Allen, *Hannah and Her Sisters* (Vintage ed., 1987), p. 121.

Florence, "Miss Bartlett only sighed, and enveloped her in a protecting embrace as she wished her good-night." Lucy submits politely, yet Forster observes that the spinster's smothering compassion gave the young girl "the sensation of a fog, and when she reached her own room she opened the window and breathed the clean night air."[2] Miss Bartlett eventually (and *so* discretely) helps Lucy see her way to truth and love in this charming novel, but literature more typically views the Protector as the victim rather than as the instigator of change. Protectors cling to the past, hoping to preserve somehow their traditional way of life, and all too often they are exploited by more impetuous lovers who take advantage of their patient devotion.

Tony Last

Evelyn Waugh's early books are bizarre, darkly comical portraits of traditional English society gone to ruin after the catastrophe of World War I. In six novels, with titles such as *Decline and Fall* and *Vile Bodies*, Waugh observes the depravity of English life in the1920's and 30's—the futile common man, the suavely ruthless Bright Young People, the obsolete aristocrats—with a detached, almost cold-blooded irony. In *A Handful of Dust*, easily the best of the lot, indeed, considered by many as one of the finest novels of the century, Waugh tells in his deadpan tone the story of Tony Last, a young Protector Guardian, married to a "devoted" Artisan wife, and described by his friends as

---

[2] E.M. Forster, *A Room with a View* (Vintage ed.), p. 15.

"one of the happiest men" in England—but who nevertheless suffers one of the most macabre downfalls in modern
fiction.

Tony Last is, indeed, the "last" representative of British
aristocratic values in Waugh's post-war England, a kind-
hearted though slightly ponderous defender of an attitude
and a way of life that had remained essentially unchanged
since the Middle Ages. He lives with his wife Brenda and
son John Andrew on the Last family estate, in a cavernous,
gloomy old manorhouse called Hetton Abbey, all battlements and clock towers and granite shafts. Tony knows that
such Gothic weightiness is woefully out of fashion after the
war (the county Guide Book calls Hetton "now devoid of
interest"), and yet as a Protector he cannot help but cherish
every detail of his ancestral home. "There was not a glazed
brick or encaustic tile that was not dear to Tony's heart,"
Waugh tells us, and to be sure, each groined ceiling, each
armorial stained glass window, each wall tapestry, each
tomb-like fireplace, each frieze of Gothic text—"all these
things with which he had grown up were a source of
constant delight and exultation to Tony; things of tender
memory and proud possession."[3]

---

[3] For purposes of his irony, Waugh deflates almost every serious
symbol in *A Handful of Dust*, and thus it should be noted that Hetton
Abbey is not a *real* thirteenth century manor, but was rebuilt in the
Gothic style by Tony's great-grandfather just fifty years earlier—or
as Waugh puts it, "It was a huge building conceived in the late
generation of the Gothic revival, when the movement had lost its
fantasy and become structurally logical and stodgy." Tony is happily
indifferent to this lack of authenticity, and the blindness of his

Protectors, most Guardians for that matter, love owning and looking after such valuable "things" of family history. To a Protector like Tony, family honor depends in large part on maintaining such accumulated treasures, such heirlooms and artifacts, and he is proud to care for these objects of the past as devotedly as he nourishes his family's current well-being. Protectors make wonderful museum curators (Keirsey calls them "natural historians"[4]), and true to form, Tony always insists on dragging his infrequent house guests to see Hetton's finest rooms and towers, explaining obscure family customs as they make their tour. But he is most delighted to display the family "collections":

> enamel, ivories, seals, snuff boxes, china, ormolu, cloisonné; they paused before each picture in the oak gallery and discussed its associations; they took out the more remarkable folios in the library and examined prints of the original buildings, manuscript account books of the old abbey, travel journals of Tony's ancestors.[5]

Protectors resist change so instinctively that they rarely cast off anything that might connect them with the past. They are the most meticulous pack rats of all the Guardians, and Tony fills his own bedroom with personal keepsakes. "He had taken nothing from the room since he had slept there," Waugh discloses, "but every year added to its contents, so

---

devotion to Hetton makes him a dear but somewhat pathetic character.

[4] David Keirsey and Marilyn Bates, *Please Understand Me*, p. 44.

[5] Evelyn Waugh, *A Handful of Dust* (Boston, 1962), p. 44. All quotations are from this edition.

that it now formed a gallery representative of every phase of his adolescence." Such carefully tended collections, even of insignificant adolescent items, are precious to all the Guardians, and differentiate them fundamentally from the other concrete temperament, the Artisans.

Artisans are just as innately drawn to the "things" of this world as the Guardians, but their natural perspective on time is different, which places them in a vitally different relation to concrete reality. Artisans have a spontaneous sense of time, and because they live so fully in the present, improvising moment-to-moment with the objects at hand, intimately and immediately in touch with the "thing in itself," they are to a great extent disconnected from the past, and seldom have the interest, or the patience, to take custody of family collections. Guardians, on the other hand, seem to have an innate regard for the past, for whatever is long-established and traditional, and they are quite honored to care for their family's heirlooms, seeing to it that they are safely shelved and regularly dusted. Guardians are not the *makers*, then, but the conscientious *caretakers* of things, and while their devotion to the past virtually precludes them from the Artisan's creativity, it also relieves them of the excitement—or the anxiety, as they would see it—of living on the cutting-edge of time. This Artisan-Guardian conflict in time perspective—the immediate and impulsive at odds with the remote and revered—is at the very heart of Tony Last's Pygmalion project in *A Handful of Dust*, as he innocently tries to preserve the medieval past in a modern Artisan world that has passed him by.

To be sure, Tony's great ambition in life is to restore Hetton to its rightful grandeur, conceding to the modern world a few minor improvements (his occasional guests complain of draughts and a shortage of bathrooms), but maintaining the general aspect and atmosphere of the place as he has always known them. Tony lies on his dais-bed on Saturday morning in Morgan le Fay (all the bedrooms are named from the Arthurian stories), and stares at the crumbling plaster in his ceiling, the tarnishing fleur-de-lis and the flaking Tudor roses, and he "resolved anew to put them right," although he is pessimistic of being able "nowadays, to find craftsmen capable of such delicate work." Despite the damp and the difficulties, however, Tony is the Protector Pygmalion at his most serene on these quiet weekend mornings, snug in the room he has slept in since he left the night nursery, surrounded by his childhood objet d'arts, and contemplating how to preserve his manor against the ravages of time. "All over England people were waking up, queasy and despondent," Waugh observes of the topsy-turvy world outside, while "Tony lay for ten minutes very happily planning the renovation of his ceiling."

In addition to these sacred objects of the past, Tony Last is determined to preserve the centuries-old way of life that Hetton stands for. When his wife Brenda begins to complain about how much it costs to maintain the Abbey, Tony is quick to defend not only its dignity, but also the inherent value of its aristocratic tradition:

We've always lived here and I hope John will be able to keep it on after me. One has a duty towards one's employees, and towards the place too. It's a defininte part of English life which would be a serious loss.[6]

Similarly, when Tony finds he must correct his son's manners (Johnny has been taunting his nanny, calling her a "silly old tart"), he delivers the boy a well-practised "homily," as Waugh calls it, about masculine noblesse oblige:

Now listen, John.... You are a gentleman. When you grow up all this house and lots of other things besides will belong to you. You must learn to speak like someone who is going to have these things and to be considerate to people less fortunate than you, particularly women. Do you understand?[7]

Another aspect of aristocratic responsibility is to maintain the appearance of Christian discipline, and although Tony is not religious himself in any deeply spiritual sense, he makes his way to the village church every Sunday morning, faithfully following "the simple, mildly ceremonious" ritual handed down from his parents and grandparents. He "invariably wore a dark suit...and a stiff white collar," sits in the massive family pew, chats affably with the vicar after the service, walks home by way of the gardners' cottages (always picking a button-hole at the hot houses), "and then, rather solemnly, drank a glass of sherry in the library."

In the same way, Guardians often find more comfort in the solemn air of Church ritual than they do in theolgy, or at

---

[6] Evelyn Waugh, *A Handful of Dust*, p. 19.
[7] Evelyn Waugh, *A Handful of Dust*, p. 25.

least they bond to the religious ideas primarily *through* the traditional ceremonies. And thus, during the formal service, Tony "inhaled the agreeable, slightly musty atmosphere and performed the familiar motions of sitting, standing, and leaning forward," and yet he pays little attention to the vicar's words, letting his thoughts wander instead to "events of the past week," or to his plans for Hetton's new lavatories. However, Tony never shirks the social ritual; he makes his appearance every Sunday, and every year he reads the Bible lessons on "Christmas Day and Harvest Thanksgiving," doing his duty to Christ as well as Demeter. And though Brenda teases him about posing as an "upright, God-fearing gentleman of the old school," he doesn't trouble himself about the harmless inconsistency: "Tony saw the joke, but this did not at all diminish the pleasure he derived from his weekly routine."

Unfortunately, Brenda is up to more mischief than just sweetly baiting her Protector husband. Brenda is a Performer Artisan (an "ESFP") who as a girl was all the rage in London society—"People used to be mad about her"—but who amazed everyone by accepting Tony Last and disappearing with him into the feudal countryside. Brenda was fond of Tony, certainly, yet as we see at the beginning of the novel, she married him for his money and for the promise of playing "Lady Brenda" at grand parties. But now, after almost seven years of quiet family life, coaxing Tony to take some interest in lively society, and watching him spend most of their money on maintaining the estate, Brenda's patience is nearly at an end. "Well it seems to me rather pointless," she grumbles, "keeping up a house this size if we don't now and then ask some other people to stay in it." And she irritates Tony further by suggesting that they abandon Hetton to visit with friends for the holidays. "Angela says will we stay for the New Year," she lets drop, barely hiding her eagerness—"it sounds an amusing party."

Tony responds at first by trying to make Brenda feel guilty for her lack of wifely devotion. "You go if you like," he sniffs, "I can't possibly get away." And then he resorts to another favorite Guardian device, the moral declaration thinly disguised as a question: "Well what sort of fun can there be in going all the way to Yorkshire in the middle of winter." Although she's impossibly bored, Brenda is not about to risk her comfortable life on such a minor point, and so acquiesces for the time being, hoping to patch things up with an appeal to Tony's economizing nature: "Darling, don't be cross. I know we aren't going....I just thought it might be fun to eat someone else's food for a bit." Satistfied with Brenda's frugal intentions, Tony relents as well, and an uneasy calm is restored, both partners keeping their Pygmalion projects at this point relatively restrained.

Some degree of conflict between saving and spending seems inevitable in Guardian-Artisan relationships, and Waugh observes brightly that such "scenes of domestic playfulness" were quite common in this one, Brenda pressing coyly for her moments of freedom, and Tony throwing up defenses to keep his life as comfortably habitual as possible. Waugh, with his cutting irony, is clearly amused by the hypocrisy of the arrangement, as he sums up the general view of the Lasts' "model" marriage:

> What with Brenda's pretty ways and Tony's good sense, it was not surprising that their friends pointed to them as a pair who were pre-eminently successful in solving the problem of getting along well together.[8]

Indeed, in good medieval style, Tony is able to keep the façade of their relationship irreproachable—Lord and Lady of the castle—while chaos lies just beneath the surface, awaiting its opportunity.

Chaos arrives quite unexpectedly one Saturday afternoon on the 3:18 train from London, in the rather unpromising figure of a young Operator Artisan (an "ESTP") named, ironically, John "Beaver." Beaver is a shallow, conniving young man who makes his living by wheedling invitations to chic luncheon parties, fashionable soirees, and occasionally to free weekends at a wealthy estate. Tony took pity on him one night at their club in London, made him a half-hearted invitation to visit Hetton, and is surprised—and terribly upset—when out of the blue he receives Beaver's telegram to pick him up at the station. Brenda, on the other hand, immediately sees in Beaver her chance to catch up on the London whirl, and so promises to entertain the young scrounger while Tony goes about his business. Brenda has the Performer's gift for spontaneous

---

[8] Evelyn Waugh, *A Handful of Dust*, p. 28.

charm, and as she listens to Beaver's witty anecdotes, and draws him out on the affaires and divorces of her old set in London ("What fun everyone seems to be having"), she quite dazzles her guest—"I'm bitching him rather," she tells her husband. On his side, Tony feels guilty for being so inhospitable, but Brenda, in true Artisan style, takes a good deal of pride in her technique:

> You know, that's a difference between us, that when some-one's awful you just run away and hide, while I actually enjoy it—making up to them and showing off to myself how well I can do it.[9]

Of course, Tony does his duty and gives Beaver the grand tour of Hetton, half hoping to bore the young man into returning early to London; but Beaver, with his Artisan's opportunistic eye, is "well practised in the art of being shown over houses," and, feeling quite at home, he cannot decide whether he is more impressed with Tony's family treasures or with his wife. Beaver happily stays the weekend playing cozy parlor games with Brenda, and he returns to London Monday morning feeling self-satisfied but somewhat baffled by his conquest.

Despite his archetypal Monitor Guardian name, Beaver is a useless young man, lacking any Guardian sense of industry, and he is just as indolent in his personal affairs, attending to life with a moral indifference that was quite fashionable at the time. Waugh's point, surely, was to emphasize in

---

[9] Evelyn Waugh, *A Handful of Dust*, p. 43.

Beaver's completely inappropriate name just how fatuous London society had become in the thirties. Waugh believed that the upper classes and the social climbers had lived through the Slump (as the Depression was called in England) in an ethical sense as well as a financial. He saw modern London society, led by characters with names such as "Viola Chasm" and "Polly Cockpurse," as existing gayly in a moral void, throwing snobbish parties and arranging casual liasons while what he called their elegant "Edwardian certainty" was crumbling around them. Artisan sensibilities, even in the traditionally Guardian English culture, had won the day, but let me emphasize that Waugh saw none of the daring sensuality of true Dionysians in these Bright Young People. Both worlds, Tony's earnestly medieval as well as London's vacuously modern, feel the sting of Waugh's wit in *A Handful of Dust,* and Beaver's ridiculous Guardian name expresses quite well the confusion of values in the novel. Brenda tells Tony, "Beaver isn't so bad. He's quite like us in some ways," but Tony, horrified, tries to keep things straight, insisting, "He's not like me."

In any event, Beaver is different enough from Tony to inspire Brenda with, not passion exactly (passion is so old-fashioned), but with a mildly scandalous sense of excitement. "What do you suppose is Mr. Beaver's sex-life?" she asks her sister, whose smile broadens with understanding: "I shouldn't know. Pretty dim I imagine....You *do* fancy him." Artisans are often cynical about other people, and Brenda certainly has no illusions about any heartfelt passion for her new conquest: "He's second rate and a snob and, I should think, as cold as a fish." She does, however, "happen to have a fancy for him," and so she soon follows Beaver up to town, rents an overdecorated little flat from his mother, and pursues what all her bored London set welcomes as "Brenda's adventure" in modern Artisan romance.

Brenda's sudden consuming interest in London may be, as her sister calls it, "hard cheese on Tony," but Tony's response to such a disruption in his married life sheds a clear light on the Protector's style of loving. Protectors may be pessimistic about most parts of life, always expecting things to go wrong, but with their mates they are exceptionally loyal and trusting, often willing to put up with a great deal that they don't approve of or even understand. Dedicated as they are to safeguarding their family, Protectors will criticize a wayward loved one, they will worry and feel forsaken, but they will also wait quite patiently for the "binge" of irresponsibility to play itself out, hoping to hold the family together for their spouse's eventual return.

At first, when Brenda proposes to stay over now and then in London ("Tony, I've found a flat"), he is not at all receptive to the idea, dismissing it with an unusually sharp retort: "Well you'd better lose it again." Brenda backs off, deciding to "attack...again later," and thus, after dinner, she curls up in her pyjamas next to Tony on the sofa, "sitting back on her heels" like a puppy to help put him in a more generous mood. Tony listens politely to Brenda's plans, quite appalled by such a disturbance to the family, and yet he seems even more concerned about the *cost* of the arrangements. Although he promises Brenda "not to brood about it," he is clearly worried that renting her a flat in London will mean putting off the improvements to Hetton that he has been saving for. But the Protector's instinct is more to satisfy his loved ones than to insist on his own desires—this is one of the Protector's most characteristic and endearing traits—and Tony soon consents to his wife's Artisan scheme, though not without a last snide remark. When Brenda gushes about the flat, "but it's *lovely*...it's all so exciting," Tony responds dryly, "You don't say so."

Naturally, Tony doesn't know the truth about Brenda's liaison in London. She tells her money-conscious husband, in a stroke of Artisan tactical brilliance, that she's taking a course in "Economics," and he tries to settle back into his normal routine at Hetton. He attends County Council meetings, discusses new tractors with his farming agent, goes to Church on Sundays—he performs all the "multifarious" duties of the aristocratic landowner. Up in London Brenda assures her sister, "The old boy's happy as a lark....He's settling down wonderfully to the new régime." And yet, in reality, Tony is lonely and miserable. He quarrels with John Andrew, he dines by himself in the library, and most pitifully of all he begins sleeping in

Brenda's empty bed. Protectors feel the loss of family unity more keenly than any other Guardians, and when Tony's duties do not fully occupy him, he finds himself wandering around Hetton, feeling guilty and anxious, finally admitting to Brenda on one of her brief visits home, "I get depressed down here all alone." However, for all his melancholy, Tony never once accuses Brenda of abandoning him, nor suspects her of infidelity. Protectors see relationships, like any other serious part of life, as a matter of history and ritual, not of spontaneous emotion, and after seven years of devoted marriage Tony simply cannot imagine his wife being involved in anything dishonorable. As Waugh explains: "He had got into a habit of loving and trusting Brenda."

However, the truth emerges tragically in the novel, and Tony's reaction to the tragedy, and to the shock of Brenda's unfaithfulness, reveals even more clearly Waugh's understanding of the male Protector Guardian. In a freak accident, John Andrew is killed while returning from his first fox-hunt; a motor bicycle backfires and bolts his horse, throwing the little boy into a ditch and breaking his neck. The death is instantaneous, and the accident itself is totally incomprehensible. Everyone at the hunt politely agrees that "it wasn't anybody's fault. It just happened." Of course, Tony is stunned by this further blow to family unity, and yet in the hours after the accident he faithfully sees to his duties as husband and father, and even as host of the hunting party. His first thought is for Brenda. She must be con-

tacted in London, he insists, though Tony is certain the
news will crush her: "you see," he confides to a friend, "I
know Brenda so well." Then there are the funeral arrangements for little John, all the "things to see to here...purely
formal." And although he admits he is in a terrible emotional "muddle," Tony takes time to make sure his guests
are comfortable and that all civilized social forms are observed:

> They had better have some luncheon before they go.
> Something cold in the dining room. I will have it with
> them....And will you put a call through to Colonel Inch and
> thank him for coming. And to Mr. Ripon's to enquire how
> Miss Ripon is. And to the vicarage and ask Mr. Tendril if I can
> see him this evening....I shall have to discuss arrangements
> with him.[10]

Not only does Tony try to minimize the disruption caused
by John Andrew's death, but he also feels he must deny its
appearance of randomness. Guardians, with their strong
belief in accountability and order, are more distressed than
any other temperament by the seeming purposelessness of
such a disaster. Guardians resist with all their sense of order
the implication of some cosmic anarchy in such an "accident," and they need to re-structure the experience as
quickly as possible to maintain their grip on reality. Thus,
as Tony awaits word from Brenda, he tries to collect the
chaotic events of the day into a structured sequence, almost
as if arranging the moments in a simple chronology is the
only way he can accept them—or perhaps even comprehend
them—as facts:

---

[10] Evelyn Waugh, *A Handful of Dust*, pp. 146-147.

It's less than four hours ago that it happened... it's odd to think that this is the same day; that it's only five hours ago they were all here at the meet having drinks....It was twenty eight minutes past twelve when I heard. I looked at my watch... It was ten to one when they brought John in...just over three hours ago... It's almost incredible, isn't it?[11]

Keirsey points out that Guardian thinking tends to be "associative, linear and additive," as opposed, say, to the Artisans' unique talent for blending or "fitting" their perceptions.[12] And certainly in this time of grief Tony's mind pursues its most characteristic mode of thought, straining to bring order out of chaos by insisting that all things have their place in a straightforward sequence of events.

For Brenda, on the other hand, the news of John Andrew's death means at last a chance to break openly with the past. Brenda comes down from London for the funeral, and Tony is encouraged that they will find each other again in their sorrow. "We're both young," he comforts her; "Of course

---

[11] Evelyn Waugh, *A Handful of Dust*, pp. 149-50.
[12] See *Portraits of Temperament*, p. 23 and pp. 58-59 for Keirsey's contrast of Artisan and Guardian consciousness. Waugh makes similar points in this scene by contrasting Tony's reaction with that of one of his Artisan guests. Mrs. Rattery, an Instrumentalist Artisan (an "ISTP") known as the "shameless blond," passes the time by immersing herself in a game of solitaire, deftly combining and recombining the cards in a search not only for Guardian sequence, but for Artisan pattern:

Mrs. Rattery sat intent over her game, moving little groups of cards adroitly backward and forwards about the table like shuttles across a loom; under her fingers order grew out of chaos; she established sequence and precedence; the symbols before her became coherent, interrelated (p. 150).

we can never forget John. He'll always be our eldest son...." But Brenda barely unpacks her bags before she returns to her flat in town, leaving Tony a letter on his breakfast tray that explains about Beaver and asks for a divorce.

Tony is stunned once again—"She's seen Beaver only twice to my knowledge," he mutters—and yet, even as the divorce proceedings begin, he remains benevolent and surprisingly protective. As a Protector, Tony cannot help taking some responsibility for the loss of his family, and he lies in bed, reliving in guilty memory the months since Beaver's visit to Hetton, "wondering where something he had said or done might have changed the course of events."

But Tony has responsibilities in the present as well, and he assumes them with a handsome formality. To avoid publicity, and to satisfy his own medieval view of women, Tony agrees to let Brenda sue as the injured party in the divorce, and he even arranges (in one of the most hilarious scenes in the novel) to stage his "infidelity" with a dance hostess at a seaside hotel. Tony's solicitor points out that this course gives Brenda claim to substantial alimony, but Tony trusts that she won't take advantage of his chivalry. Tony assures his solicitor that he and his wife have agreed on a fair settlement, and "Lady Brenda's word is quite good enough."

Let me point out that, though Tony behaves quite gallantly in the proceedings, he is acting more out of good-breeding than from any lingering love for Brenda. Guardians make passionate attachments, of course, but they also consider marriage as an agreement to be honored, a legally binding contract. And thus, though Tony tries to be dependable and civilized throughout the negotiations ("I'm doing exactly what Brenda wanted"), he finds it unforgivable that his wife has reneged on their vows, and he insists he will not have her back. "That's vindictive," Brenda's older brother charges, trying to arrange a reconciliation; but Tony answers politely, and in his matter-of-fact tone: "No, I just couldn't feel the same about her again."

In a larger sense, Brenda's unfaithfulness has also shaken Tony's confidence in the stability of his time-honored English way of life—or as Waugh puts it, describing the Protector Guardian's deepest disillusionment:

> for a month now he had lived in a world suddenly bereft of order; it was as though the whole reasonable and decent constitution of things, the sum of all he had experienced or learned to expect, were an inconspicuous, inconsiderable object mislaid somewhere on the dressing table; no outrageous circumstance in which he found himself, no new mad thing brought to his notice could add a jot to the all-encompassing chaos that shrieked about his ears.[13]

And so, after Brenda reneges again, increasing her demands in the divorce settlement to a truly impossible sum of money (which Tony clarifies as "I should give up Hetton in order to buy Beaver for Brenda"), he has had quite enough.

---

[13] Evelyn Waugh, *A Handful of Dust*, p. 189.

Calmly but firmly, Tony refuses to act any longer as the defendant in the divorce; he vows to deny Brenda a farthing in alimony, will drag her through a public trial if necessary; and to wash his hands of the entire business, he books passage as an assistant explorer on a two-man expedition to the Amazon jungle.

No second hand summary can do justice to the inspired irony of the last two chapters of *A Handful of Dust*, as Waugh brilliantly juxtaposes scenes of Brenda's tribulations in London society with Tony's calamitous trip to find a Lost City in the uncharted wilds of Brazil. Let me only say that Tony's journey is no impulsive, out-of-character Artisan adventure for him. On the contrary, in good Guardian form Tony believes that a lengthy trip to clear the air "seemed to be the conduct expected of a husband in his circumstances." And more importantly, let me add that Tony's search for the Lost City—called "the Shining" by the Indians—is in fact a search for his own lost way of life. "He had a clear picture of [the City] in his mind," Waugh discloses,

> It was Gothic in character, all vanes and pinnacles, gargoyles, battlements, groining and tracery, pavilions and terraces, a transfigured Hetton.[14]

In other words, Tony's expedition into the jungle is really a Protector Guardian's quest for a shimmering, immaculate past—a medieval castle keep without modern betrayals and

---

[14] Evelyn Waugh, *A Handful of Dust*, p. 222.

conveniences, without Brendas and Beavers and indoor lavatories. And in a dark and dreadful way Waugh makes Tony's dream come true.

Right from the start, the expedition has its difficulties, and when the native guides scatter in fear, and the one veteran explorer drowns searching for help, Tony is left to wander alone in the jungle, into the dreaded Pie-Wie Indian territory. Tony is found burning up with malaria by an ageless recluse in that corner of the jungle, an old Inspector Guardian (an "ISTJ") named Mr. Todd. Mr. Todd nurses Tony through his fever, restores him to health and to strength, but gradually reveals that he has no intention of returning him to the modern world. Mr. Todd's only entertainment is an old, decaying *Complete Works of Charles Dickens*, and (illiterate himself) his quietly perverse desire is to keep Tony trapped on his small plantation as his private reader. Tony pleads with and then threatens Mr. Todd for his release, but the old man just smiles and grips his shotgun, and asks politely for a few chapters more. And when a search party finally penetrates to Mr. Todd's little kingdom, the old man quickly drugs Tony and hides him out of the way—then gives them Tony's pocket watch as proof that Tony is dead, but also indicating more symbolically that Tony's concern with the world of time is over for ever.

Mr. Todd oversees his remote domain like a feudal lord, and his hold on Tony is as relentless as Waugh's irony. As a Guardian, Tony always wanted to live in a protected, traditional past, a sentimental yet morally earnest England such as Dickens captured in his novels—indeed, Tony's crotchety Aunt Frances used to sneer that Hetton Abbey looked like it belonged in Dickens—and Mr. Todd rather morbidly grants him his wish. Todd (or "todt") means "death" in Dutch (the old man is Dutch on his father's side), and in many ways, as I have said, the stasis of death or of winter seems naturally fulfilling to the Guardians, more in keeping with their cautious sensibilities than the chaos of spring. The famous opening lines of T.S. Eliot's *The Waste Land* express this conservative Guardian preference for the security of Demeter over the orgy of Dionysus:

> April is the cruellest month, breeding
> Lilacs out of the dead land, mixing
> Memory and desire, stirring
> Dull roots with spring rain.
> Winter kept us warm, covering
> Earth in forgetful snow, feeding
> A little life with dried tubers.[15]

And thus, even though he protests formally, Tony must slowly accept what is clearly the natural extension—ad absurdum—of his entire way of life. Tony's uniquely Guardian doom is to endure a living death in the timeless jungle, trapped in the feudal past and bound for life in solemn ritual, reading Dickens over and over again to a madman.[16]

---

[15] T.S. Eliot, *The Waste Land*, ll. 1-7.

[16] In a wonderful (and completely coincidental) twist on Tony's fate, Dr. Milton Erickson describes how he treated an insomniac by having the client get up and read English literature when he couldn't sleep. The client's sleep pattern improved quickly under such a benevolent ordeal, and he told Erickson a year later that, "I've got a

As you may know, Waugh took his title "A Handful of Dust" from *The Waste Land*, and the novel draws on the poem in many ingenious ways. Eliot, in his most ecclesiastical voice, promises his readers early in the poem to explore the terror and dessication at the heart of modern life—"I will show you fear in a handful of dust"—and on the most obvious level Waugh's novel sounds a similiar warning to modern man. Eliot and to a lesser extent Waugh himself saw life after World War I as barren and devoid of meaning. Modern man was cut off from the ancient springs of creativity; the Dionysian gods that granted us fertility and rebirth were dead, and modern life was reduced to mechanical motions on an arid plain. Eliot deeply despaired of this exhaustion of the spirit and the imagination, and sought salvation, even at the end of *The Waste Land*, in the life-giving waters of religion, philosophy and art.

But at this point, in their early writings at least, Eliot and Waugh part company. Waugh in *A Handful of Dust* might share Eliot's despair of the modern world, but he will not allow his characters to find refuge in what Walter Allen calls Eliot's "fructifying"[17] mythologies. Waugh's criticism of modern life is at once shallower and more pitiless than Eliot's. Waugh allows no escape in *A Handful of Dust*: Tony's Guardian dreams of ancient nobility seem nearly as

---

whole set of Dickens waiting in case my insomnia comes back." See Jay Haley, ed., *Conversations with Milton H. Erickson, M.D.*, (Triangle Press, 1985), Vol. 1, p. 59.

[17] Walter Allen, *The Modern Novel in Britain and the United States* (New York, 1965), p. 211.

ridiculous as Brenda's modern Artisan depravity, and are met with an even more undeserving punishment. In Waugh's macabre comedy, virtually nothing is undefiled— not even the imagined past—and perhaps Tony understood this most clearly in the delirium of his fever. "I will tell you what I have learned in the forest, where time is different," he rambles to Mr. Todd, barely coherent but strangely perceptive; "There is no City. Mrs. Beaver has covered it with chromium plating and converted it into flats.... Very suitable for base love...under the fallen battlements."

Tess Durbeyfield

Although Tony Last ends up victimized by both his wife and by a lunatic Dickensian in *A Handful of Dust*, the novel is essentially a comical look at the Protector's interpersonal predicaments, and our delight in Evelyn Waugh's irreverent wit rather takes the edge off the injustice of Tony's fate. Life and love can treat the Protector more cruelly, however, and for this more tragical view I want to turn briefly to Thomas Hardy's sorrowful novel, *Tess of the D'Urbervilles*.

Western literature often reserves the harsher role of interpersonal victim for the female Protector Guardian. Indeed, there is something of the victim in the very nature of the Guardian's totem goddess, Demeter, who protects the abundance of the fields but is ritually sacrificed in the harvest. Sir James Frazer in *The Golden Bough* describes the wide-spread practice in farming cultures of killing the goddess in animal form at the close of the threshing:

> In one or other of these [animal] shapes the corn-spirit is often believed to be present in the corn, and to be caught and killed in the last sheaf. As the corn is being cut the animal flees before the reapers... to be killed by the last stroke of sickle or scythe... to be caught in the last sheaf threshed.[18]

And this same scene is played out in *Tess of the D'Urbervilles*, although without any sense of celebration, as the merciless modern reaping-machine makes its way around the "fertile and sheltered" fields near Tess's girlhood home:

> The narrow lane of stubble encompassing the field grew wider with each circuit, and the standing corn was reduced to a smaller area as the morning wore on. Rabbits, hares, snakes, rats, mice, retreated inwards as into a fastness, unaware of the ephemeral nature of their refuge and of the doom that awaited them later in the day, when, their covert shrinking to a more and more horrible narrowness, they were huddled together, friends and foes, till the last few yards of upright wheat fell also under the teeth of the unerring reaper, and they were every one put to death by the sticks and stones of the harvesters.[19]

In many ways this scene of slowly circling death sets the pattern for Hardy's entire account of Tess's short and piteous life. Tess is actually referred to as "Demeter" in the

---

[18] Sir James Frazer, *The Golden Bough, A Study in Magic and Religion*, abridged edition (New York, 1943), pp. 447-448.

[19] Thomas Hardy, *Tess of the D'Urbervilles* (Signet ed., 1964), p. 103. All quotations are from this edition.

novel, and Hardy describes her with many images of helpless animals and birds; to be sure, Tess's simple desire throughout the novel is to find some place of refuge, some haven or "nest" as Hardy often calls it, to provide her peace and protection from the doom that is closing its fingers around her. Thus Tess cries to her implacable Artisan lover, "Once victim, always victim—that's the law!" and Hardy describes the hopeless look on her face as "the...sparrow's gaze before its captor twists its neck." I don't intend to discuss all the painful variations of Hardy's theme in *Tess of the D'Urbervilles*, but Keirsey maintains that the Guardians are the most fatalistic and pessimistic of all the temperaments,[20] and I know of no novel that better captures this depressive side of the Protector's nature.

Even before the ruinous events of her own life begin, Tess's outlook on life is, in a word, dismal. Though only a teenager when we first meet her in the novel, Tess already views her young existence with a "yellow melancholy," and she is convinced that the earth is a "blighted" star, with the night wind in the trees sounding to her like "the sigh of some immense sad soul." Her parents are indigent village Artisans—her father a shiftless, tipsy Promoter (an "ESTP"), and her mother Joan a cheerful Performer (an "ESFP"), with a gift for singing and having babies—and Tess is often the only one responsible enough to fend for her little brothers and sisters, "six helpless creatures," as Hardy calls them, "who had never been asked if they wished for life...on such hard conditions." Indeed, late one

---

[20] David Keirsey, *Portraits of Temperament*, p. 48 and p. 59.

night, when her father is too drunk to take the hives to market, Tess in true Protector style "thought that she could take upon herself the entire load," and offers to drive the family wagon. But when Tess fails in her duty and the family horse is killed in a road accident, she loads herself instead with a crushing self-reproach.

Guardians in general take their responsibilities more seriously than the other temperaments; they expect such tireless dependability from themselves—at all times and in all situations—that even their most innocent mistakes can weigh heavily upon them. Thus, while her Artisan parents accept the loss simply as a part of life—"We must take the ups wi' the downs" her mother tells her—Tess insists on taking all the blame herself, crying, "'Tis all my doing—all mine....No excuse for me—none." Just the day before, Tess had joined in the village May-day festival celebrating spring's fertility; but now, shaken back into her Protector's more autumnal view, she sees how frivolous was her optimism: "Why, I danced and laughed only yesterday....To think I was such a fool!"

Not only is Tess's guilt exaggerated (she "regarded herself in the light of a murderess"), but so is her desire to make some sort of reparation for what she insists is her terrible crime. Guardians, as Keirsey points out, structure their lives largely on an economic model, their thought running naturally along lines of debit and credit,[21] and I would extend this even to their sense of morality. As a failed

---

[21] David Keirsey, *Portraits of Temperament*, pp. 44-45 and pp. 55-56.

Protector, one who has jeopardized her family's security, Tess makes a simple audit of her responsibilities. "The oppressive sense of the harm she had done" has put her grievously in debt to her parents, she believes, and she is determined to find some means of paying them back.

Tess vows to find the money somewhere for a new horse, but at this point her mother proposes an ill-fated scheme. Joan Durbeyfield, with her Artisan optimism, wants Tess to present herself to the wealthy branch of the family—the noble D'Urbervilles—hoping that Tess's modesty will win their compassion, and her beauty perhaps a rich husband. Tess is mortified by her mother's shamelessness, and resists the idea. "I'd rather try to get work," she pleads, but her sense of obligation is so compelling that she puts aside her pride and consents finally to do as her mother wishes, sadly aware that "Every day seemed to throw upon her young shoulders more of the family burdens." Tess's decision to play the part of poor relation is just one in a series of well-intentioned but disastrous steps she takes in *Tess of the D'Urbervilles*. Guardians believe stubbornly that if anything *can* go wrong in life it will, and Tess's every experience in the novel seems to bear out this unhappy expectation.

Tess soon makes her approach to the grand D'Urberville mansion, and she even meets her "rich young man," Alec Stoke-D'Urberville, the heir of the nuveau riche banking family which has bought up the defunct D'Urberville family name and rebuilt the estate. Alec greets Tess on the massive front lawns, listens with amusement to her story, and promises out of "the prodigality of his bounty" to come to her rescue. But as fate would have it the generosity she receives at his hands is inevitably her undoing.

Alec is a swank, cocky Promoter Artisan (an "ESTP"), notorious for having his favorites among the local farming-girls, and Hardy's initial description of him leaves little doubt about his capacity for evil:

> He had an almost swarthy complexion, with full lips, badly molded, though red and smooth, above which was a well-groomed black moustache with curled points....Despite the touches of barbarism in his contours, there was a singular force in the gentleman's face and in his bold rolling eye.[22]

Alec is immediately aroused by Tess's beauty and vulnerability, and in a scene of astonishing sexual evocativeness for Hardy's late-Victorian readers, he strolls with Tess through the luxuriant gardens, heaping her "little basket" with rose blossoms, tucking the long stems into her hat and her bosom. And then he invites her to eat her fill of early summer strawberries:

> ...he stood up and held [the fruit] by the stem to her mouth.
> "No—no!" she said quickly, putting her fingers between his hand and her lips. "I would rather take it in my own hand."
> "Nonsense!" he insisted, and in a slight distress she parted her lips and took it in.[23]

---

[22] Thomas Hardy, *Tess of the D'Urbervilles*, p. 51.
[23] Thomas Hardy, *Tess of the D'Urbervilles*, p. 53.

In many ways, this sexually suggestive interplay (Tess surrendering "half-pleased, half-reluctant," and Alec smoking his cigar "with a pleased gleam in his face") prefigures the climax of this first phase of Tess's relationship with her Dionysian benefactor. Alec arranges for Tess to work on the estate, he spends several months trying to break down her virtuous resistance, and then finally, as the year turns toward Demeter's autumn, he rides with Tess into the fog-shrouded woods, makes a "nest for her in the deep mass of dead leaves," and has his way with her. However, even in their more symbolic initial interview, Hardy makes it clear that Tess's fate is sealed:

> Tess Durbeyfield did not divine, as she innocently looked down at the roses in her bosom, that there behind the blue narcotic haze was potentially the "tragic mischief" of her drama—one who stood fair to be the blood-red ray in the spectrum of her young life.[24]

Indeed, Hardy steps out of the narrative, as he often does at the end of his chapters, and broadens his point to express the Guardian's darkest fears about the hopelessly adverse nature of human relationships:

> Had [Tess] perceived this meeting's import, she might have asked why she was doomed to be seen and coveted that day by the wrong man and not by some other man, the right and desired one....In the ill-judged execution of the well-judged plan of things, the call seldom produces the comer, the man to love rarely coincides with the hour for loving.[25]

---

[24] Thomas Hardy, *Tess of the D'Urbervilles*, p. 54.
[25] Thomas Hardy, *Tess of the D'Urbervilles*, pp. 54-55.

Tess's submission to Alec, both at their first meeting and then later in the woods (Hardy describes it as "she obeyed like one in a dream"), is surprising behavior on her part, seemingly not in keeping with her stern, conscientious Guardian temperament. But the mystery is even more puzzling. When Hardy resumes the story after the night in the woods, Tess has just left Alec, and is walking the road back home, weighed down and weeping with guilt for her loss of innocence. But Hardy is careful to point out that this scene takes place not the next morning, but several weeks after her disastrous night ride, inferring that she has stayed on with Alec all this time. And further, by alluding to the intimate terms of her relationship with Alec during these weeks (Alec kisses Tess goodbye, "half perfunctorily, half as if zest had not yet quite died out"), Hardy suggests that Tess was not entirely innocent in the seduction.[26] The question, of course, is why Tess succumbs to Alec's pressure and gives herself up to such a conniving Artisan lover, even if unwillingly and only for a short while. The answers must be speculative, but they offer us an important perspective on the female Protector Guardian's emotional nature.

On the surface of it, Hardy attributes Tess's surrender to her naiveté. "I didn't understand your meaning till it was too late," she tells Alec as she leaves him, and certainly a sixteen year old village girl is vulnerable in the hands of a worldly Artisan. But I think a more compelling explanation

---

[26] Roman Polanski's film *Tess* develops this point well beyond the novel's subtle evidence, suggesting that Tess actually lives with Alec as his mistress.

of Tess's submission to Alec is found in psychologist Franz Alexander's work on emotional logic. Alexander argues that retentive personalities (hoarding and protecting Conservator Guardians like Tess) are likely to base their behavior on a number of what he calls "emotional syllogisms," powerful "guilt or superego reactions," one of which convinces the Guardian: "Because I received so much, I must give something in return."[27] Alec is clearly not the man of Tess's dreams in the novel, but he *has* given her a home and a job, and on the night he carries her into the woods, he tells her about the new horse he has given her father, and of the toys he has bought for her brothers and sisters. Tess weeps when she hears of his generosity, confessing "It—hampers me so." And when Alec presses her, "Tessy, don't you love me ever so little now?" she reluctantly admits, "I'm grateful." There is no evidence in the novel that Tess loves Alec in any tender, heartfelt way, but it appears that she is "stirred to confused surrender awhile," as Hardy discreetly puts it, overpowered by the same profound burden of debt that she felt with her parents, and that so often governs the Protector Guardian's relationships.

In any event, Tess stays with Alec until she is overwhelmed with guilt ("I...so loathe and hate myself for my weakness"), and then she leaves without telling him that she carries his child. The baby, whom she names "Sorrow," is

---

[27] Franz Alexander, "The Logic of Emotions and Its Dynamic Background," *International Journal of Psychoanalysis*, 16:1935, p. 407.

sickly and dies soon after birth, but Tess is doomed from that time forward to wander what she envisions as "a long and stony highway...without aid and with little sympathy," toward her final surrender to Alec at the end of the novel—and then to her violent and deadly break for freedom. Tess's fate could not be more tragic. In bitter conflict with her Protector's powerful nesting instinct, as well as with her Protector's inherent dread of social isolation, Tess must live the rest of her life as a virtual outcast from her family, indeed from all respectable Victorian society. "She would pay," Hardy warns his readers, "to the uttermost farthing" for her sin.

Tess of the D'Urbervilles is a long, elegiac novel, perhaps more broadly sociological in its intention than psychological. To be sure, Hardy laments the innocent Guardian's helplessness at the hands of Artisan love, but in Hardy's larger view Tess's fate represents the destruction of an entire way of life in England at the end of the nineteenth century. Hardy suggests that as surely as Alec rapes and ruins Tess in the novel, the modern world of mechanical reapers and "red glutton" steam threshers, of bourgeois industrialism and callous opportunism, is ravaging and leaving for dead the agrarian village culture that Hardy explored so faithfully in his novels. Hardy saw the simple life of the "work-folk," managing the animals and the fields, worshipping at Demeter's humble altar, as being uprooted to make way for the ruthless twentieth century, and he mourns its passing in the destruction of Tess Durbeyfield.

But again, for all the malevolent historical forces at work in the novel, Hardy clearly understands the temperamental basis of the female Guardian's attraction to the male Artisan. So heavily burdened with what Hardy calls the "moral hobgoblins" of her "conventional aspect," Tess is fascinated almost against her will by Alec's freedom of action and sense of masculine power, and she is virtually blind to his manipulative nature. "My eyes were dazed by you for a little," Tess confesses to him, "and that was all." Though Tess does not appear to be addicted, in Robin Norwood's sense,[28] to Alec's mistreatment of her, she is inexorably drawn to him, finally to her own destruction, just as Guardian women in general all too often find themselves in the power of Pygmalion men who exploit them cruelly.

Mrs. Ramsay

Not all Protector women are this vulnerable in their relationships, of course, nor are their men always this villainous. Indeed, the female Protector most often brings a welcome sense of warmth and stability to her marriage, particularly if her husband is a seclusive ("introverted") Artisan or Rational, lost as these types often seem to be in their respective worlds of action or intellect. In such a marriage, the female Protector can be the one, vital source of nurturing and family unity for her seemingly discon-

---

[28] Robin Norwood, *Women Who Love Too Much* (Pocket ed., 1986), pp. 61-62.

nected spouse, a role and a relationship that Virginia Woolf portrays with remarkable sensitivity in her novel, *To the Lighthouse.*

Virginia Woolf's novels are psychological portraits in the purest sense. She develops her stories not so much by plotting a series of external events as by tracing the flow of thoughts and feelings in a single character, or among a small group of interrelated characters, each reacting in turn to a series of apparently insignificant occurences, utterances, or perceptions. One by one, Woolf drops a handful of plain pebbles into the pool of awareness in her characters, and then she relates in the most delicate detail, and in her poetic stream-of-consciousness style, how far the ripples spread in time and space, how they lap against each other, uncovering memories, clarifying relationships, washing clean her characters' understanding of each other and of their own lives. Thus, the events of the first half of *To The Lighthouse* take place on a single September evening, some years before World War I, and the story expands from a single interchange between husband and wife. But from these modest starting points Woolf sets in motion a rich and profoundly intimate analysis of a Protector Guardian-Strategist Rational (an "ISFJ"-"INTJ") marriage.

"Yes, of course, if it's fine tomorrow." *To the Lighthouse* begins with these soothing words from Mrs. Ramsay, encouraging her son James that, yes, the long-awaited family expedition to the nearby lighthouse has every chance of taking place. As her opening words suggest, Mrs. Ramsay is an enduring mother-figure in the novel, a source of seemingly archetypal nurturing and protection, even admitting at one point, "She would have liked always to have had a baby. She was happiest carrying one in her arms." Though fifty years old, with eight children (little James is only six), she is serene and still extraordinarily beautiful, and, as she sits with her son in the open window facing the sea, knitting stockings for the lighthouse keeper's little boy, one old friend on the terrace actually describes the scene in near-religious terms: "mother and child," he thinks to himself, sit framed as in a medieval icon, "objects of universal veneration."

Whether Protector or Madonna, Mrs. Ramsay is concerned and comforting to all in her world—her family, her house-guests, even the poor villagers in the Hebrides where the Ramsays spend their pre-war holidays—but she is particularly devoted to taking care of the men in her life. Very simply, she believes, "she had the whole of the other sex under her protection." Demeter is often thought of as the protector of married life, and Mrs. Ramsay has always, and without apology, insisted on the importance of husband and children. "They all must marry," she urges her female friends, as well as her own daughters; "there was no disputing this: an unmarried woman...has missed the best of life." To be sure, Mrs. Ramsay is often accused of coercing her friends into marriage—"Wishing to dominate, wishing to interfere, making people do as she wished"— and she blushes to admit that, at times, "she was driven on, too quickly...to say that people must marry; people must have children." Her daughters, of course, resist her Pygmalion project and dream of more exciting, modern lives, "not always taking care of some man or other." But Mrs. Ramsay has always preferred the humbler satisfactions of being a wife and mother, and "for her own part she would never for a single second regret her decision, evade difficulties, or slur over duties." Thus, as the novel opens, Mrs. Ramsay knows that little James has his heart set on a trip "to the lighthouse," and even though clearly a storm is blowing up, her Protector's duty is to let him hope as long as possible.

"'But,' said his father, stopping outside of the drawing-room window, 'it won't be fine.'" Mr. Ramsay's words, sharpened with his Rational arrogance and asserting "his own accuracy of judgement," intrude into the gentle rapport of mother and child and rudely discompose the September evening. Mr. Ramsay is a University philosopher (an epistemologist, more specifically—his work is about "subject and object and the nature of reality"), and he has little patience with his wife's kindhearted disregard for objective evidence. He often lectures Mrs. Ramsay about how she teaches her children "to exaggerate," while he takes an austere pride that,

> What he said was true. It was always true. He was incapable of untruth; never...altered a disagreeable word to suit the pleasure or convenience of any mortal being.[29]

---

[29] Virginia Woolf, *To the Lighthouse* (Harvest ed., 1955), pp. 10-11. All quotations are from this edition.

Mr. Ramsay is sixty years old, with his best work well behind him, and with his eccentricities growing on him alarmingly: he storms back and forth on the terrace, for example, reciting verses from "The Charge of the Light Brigade." In keeping with the poem, he sees himself as a last bastion against muddled thinking and sentimental hypocrisy, a heroic thinker doomed to failure, but standing with "his intensity of mind...on his little ledge facing the dark of human ignorance." And in these first pages, when he hears his wife in essence deluding their son with her pretty promises, he feels nothing less than an intellectual duty to stop at the window and correct her.

Satisfied that he has re-established objective truth, Mr. Ramsay launches back onto the terrace, booming out happily (to himself, but for all to hear) "Some one had blundered," and Mrs. Ramsay calms her resentment and resumes her Protector's role with little James, hoping to restore their tranquility. "'Perhaps you will wake up and find the sun shining and the birds singing,' she said compassionately, smoothing the little boy's hair." Mrs. Ramsay deplores such family strife and division, especially in public, and fully expects her husband to soften his tyrannical position. She even offers him the opportunity to relent, asking him gently when he stops again at the window: "How did he know" the storm was coming; didn't "the wind often change?" But Mr. Ramsay this time shakes his head angrily at "the extraordinary irrationality of her remark," and, fuming more generally at "the folly of

women's minds," he stamps his foot in frustration and
hisses, "Damn you." Mrs. Ramsay can only keep her
Protector's thoughts to herself and bow beneath his cold
rage:

> To pursue truth with such astonishing lack of consideration for
> other people's feelings, to rend the thin veils of civilization so
> wantonly, so brutally, was to her so horrible an outrage of
> human decency that, without replying, dazed and blinded, she
> bent her head as if to let the pelt of jagged hail, the drench of
> dirty water, bespatter her unrebuked. There was nothing to be
> said.[30]

Rationals pride themselves on maintaining their composure
in the heat of argument, but at times, caught up in their
logic, they will attack an opponent quite viciously, even if
the "opponent" happens to be their spouse. And in this case
Mr. Ramsay realizes he has lost control and said too much,
and he backs down stiffly, "ashamed of his petulance,"
finally promising his wife to check with the Coastguards
about the weather. Mrs. Ramsay gives in as well, assuring
her husband that she was only trying to do her duty and
plan the trip properly. "She was quite ready to take his word
for it," she insists, "only then they need not cut sandwiches,
that was all" (although in her own mind she is not quite so
conciliatory, and grouses silently about her unappreciated
family burdens: "They came to her...all day long with this
and that; one wanting this, another that"). However, with
husband and wife making this honest effort at accomoda-
tion, neither holding out for a Pygmalion victory, the

---

[30] Virginia Woolf, *To the Lighthouse*, p. 51.

sudden storm in their marriage, unlike the storm brewing outside, seems to pass without serious damage. Or as Mrs. Ramsay gratefully puts it: "domesticity triumphed; custom crooned its soothing rhythm."

Although an embarrassed peace is restored in the relationship, the aftertaste of the exchange affects Mr. and Mrs. Ramsay deeply and, in Virginia Woolf's delicate fashion, they withdraw into their internal worlds, diverging into separate introspections about their marriage and their lives. As a seclusive Rational, Mr. Ramsay needs his "privacy...to regain his equilibrium," and so striding off to be by himself he embarks on an alternately heroic and self-critical evaluation of his intellect, and of how his wife and children ("a hen, straddling her wings out in protection of a covey of little chicks") might have kept him from the full greatness of his genius. (I will follow his dreams and his dismay in *The Pygmalion Project, Volume Four: The Rational.*) For her part, Mrs. Ramsay resumes her knitting and begins a long, intimate consideration of her own life as a Protector wife and mother.

Almost at once Mrs. Ramsay's attention drifts to the sound of the sea, and the surge of the waves floods her with recognition of the two sides of her Protector's nature. On the one hand, the Protector lovingly nurtures her family, and for Mrs. Ramsay,

> the monotonous fall of the waves on the beach...for the most part beat a measured and soothing tatoo to her thoughts and seemed consolingly to repeat over and over again as she sat with the children the words of some old cradle song,

murmured by nature, "I am guarding you—I am your support."[31]

On the other hand, the Protector, no matter how comforting, is never able to ignore for very long the apprehension of life's misery, and so to Mrs. Ramsay the crashing sea

> suddenly and unexpectedly, especially when her mind raised itself slightly from the task at hand, had no such kindly meaning, but like a ghostly roll of drums remorselessly beat the measure of life, made one think of the destruction of the island and its engulfment in the sea, and warned her whose day had slipped past in one quick doing after another that it was all ephemeral as a rainbow.[32]

Here again are Demeter's two eternally conflicting moods: the dependable security of home and family giving way to the inexorable awareness of winter's destruction.

Mrs. Ramsay's interior monologue shifts back and forth between these two disparate voices in her nature, providing us a rare opportunity to listen in on the workings of Guardian consciousness. Mrs. Ramsay thinks of her married life as "two different notes, one high, one low, struck together," and certainly her mental life sounds the same duality of tone. Thus, even before her husband hurries off to his private inventory, as he stands outside the window asking with his every look for sympathy and forgiveness, Mrs. Ramsay feels all the pride of her maternity. "Boasting of her capacity to surround and protect," Mrs. Ramsay

---

[31] Virginia Woolf, *To the Lighthouse*, p. 27.
[32] Virginia Woolf, *To the Lighthouse*, pp. 27-28

assured him (as a nurse carrying a light across a dark room assures a fractious child), that it was real; the house was full; the garden blowing. If he put implicit faith in her, nothing should hurt him; however deep he buried himself or climbed high, not for a second should he find himself without her.[33]

Nourished and reassured ("like a child who drops off satisfied"), Mr. Ramsay leaves to follow his own thoughts, but Mrs. Ramsay begins immediately to fret "ignobly in the wake of her exaltation," sinking into sadness about her husband's weakness and his dependency on her. Protectors are naturally modest about themselves, and Mrs. Ramsay "did not like, even for a second, to feel finer than her husband." She suddenly hears the two notes of her marriage sound "a dismal flatness," and she goes on to contemplate "the inadequacy of human relationships, that the most perfect was flawed."

Expanding further, Mrs. Ramsay thinks of how difficult and disappointing life is, and how she has condemned eight children to go through it all—"love and ambition and being wretched alone in dreary places"—and she wonders why must they grow up and lose all the happiness of childhood? For life to Mrs. Ramsay—and this precisely describes the Guardian attitude—is "a sort of transaction...in which she was on one side, and life was on another, and she was always trying to get the better of it, as it was of her." At times, when she has a moment alone, a truce seems to settle over the fray, but for the most part, "she must admit that she

---

[33] Virginia Woolf, *To the Lighthouse*, p. 60.

felt this thing that she called life terrible, hostile, and quick to pounce on you if you gave it a chance." Indeed, she wonders (knitting again, consumed in thought),

> How could any Lord have made this world?...there is not reason, order, justice: but suffering, death, the poor. There was no treachery too base for the world to commit; she knew that. No happiness lasted; she knew that.[34]

Mr. Ramsay has often become impatient with her for such irrational pessimism. "Why take such a gloomy view of life?" he has corrected her; "it is not sensible." But as she knits and thinks of the world's sorrows and cruelties, she purses her lips, stiffening her face once again into the stern composure she assumes "in the presence of her old antagonist, life."

Mrs. Ramsay claims one victory in her struggle with life, however, and as her thinking flows around this point, she clarifies even more about the Protector's internal nature. Mrs. Ramsay reflects that, in certain private moments, she is able to shed all the urgency and obligation in her life, and come to rest in what can only be described as a Protector's idea of paradise: "There was freedom, there was peace, there was, most welcome of all, a summoning together, a resting on a platform of stability." Keirsey explains that in their leisure time, Guardians enjoy "restfully taking surcease from their obligations,"[35] and in her rare moments alone, Mrs. Ramsay

---

[34] Virginia Woolf, *To the Lighthouse*, p. 98.
[35] David Keirsey, *Portraits of Temperament*, p. 61.

lost the fret, the hurry, the stir; and there rose to her lips always some exclamation of triumph over life when things came together in this peace, this rest, this eternity.[36]

Let me point out that all the temperaments occasionally find these moments of calm at the center of the storm, though each in its own way. Artisans experience periods of unconscious oneness with the physical world, Idealists feel a mysterious identification with all of existence, and Rationals are able to glimpse the most elegant solutions to profound intellectual problems. And though Virginia Woolf's lyrical prose makes Mrs. Ramsay's peaceful unity sound rather transcendental and Idealistic, her uniquely Guardian recognition is of a stable, unchanging sense of order beneath the confusion of everyday events—of an essential reliability at the heart of life:

> there is a coherence in things, a stability; something, she meant, is immune from change, and shines out... in the face of the flowing, the fleeting, the spectral... so that again... she had the feeling... of peace, of rest. Of such moments, she thought, the thing is made that endures.[37]

Like Tony Last searching for a "Shining" Hetton in the Amazon jungle, or Tess Durbeyfield longing for a protected "nest" in the doomed Wessex countryside, Mrs. Ramsay's deepest joy is to find this tranquil, luminous center somewhere in the pull and confusion of her family life, to grasp "the thing that mattered" in the flow of time, "to detach it; separate it off; clean it of all... the odds and ends

---

36 Virginia Woolf, *To the Lighthouse*, p. 96.
37 Virginia Woolf, *To the Lighthouse*, p. 158.

of things, and so hold it before her." This determination to preserve her own sense of dignity, not to be entirely lost in the rush of time and events, expresses the Protector Guardian's fundamental belief in personal stability, and suggests that Mrs. Ramsay is, in one sense, a lighthouse herself. Indeed, as the evening lengthens, and Mrs. Ramsay watches the first flashes of the lighthouse beacon sweep through the dusk, she recognizes herself in "the long steady stroke...which was her stroke," and she understands even more clearly her Protector's instinct to maintain her steadfast light in the approaching night of storm.[38]

Mrs. Ramsay's extraordinary vision of her Guardian stability underlying the discord of life not only settles her own mind, but eventually leads her a step further, into re-establishing the stability of her marriage. Mrs. Ramsay knows that if she and her husband are truly to come together again, she—as the Protector and as the female— must see to it, and late that night, after hostessing dinner and tucking the smaller children in bed, she finally finds her moment. In a last scene of wonderful subtlety and wisdom, Mrs. Ramsay joins her husband in the drawing-room, and the two of them sit quietly reading. Mr. Ramsay is absorbed in his novel and clearly wants to be left alone, to brood in his "masculine intelligence." But on her side Mrs. Ramsay vaguely wants "something more," wants (she realizes) to break the awkward silence and to begin their reconciliation.

---

[38] On another level altogether, this coming storm might be seen as World War I, a time of terrifying chaos and destruction that brings tragic changes to the Ramsay family in the second and third parts of the novel.

Mrs. Ramsay knows she must secure her husband's cooperation—"She wanted him to say something," she knows inside, "wishing only to hear his voice"—but as a non-directive Guardian she cannot command his participation in any overt or decisive way. And so, putting her book aside to take up her knitting, she looks at her husband lost in his reading, and urges him in her thoughts: "Do say something." Mr. Ramsay remains aloof at first, but as if responding to the intensity of his wife's silent call, he slowly begins to rouse from his private world:

> But through the crepuscular walls of their intimacy, for they were drawing together, involuntarily, coming side by side, quite close, she could feel his mind like a raised hand shadowing her mind.[39]

Mr. Ramsay finally looks up and breaks the silence, observing precisely, "you won't finish that stocking tonight," but the stir of emotion in his voice and in his eyes betrays another message, one that both thrills and threatens the innately reserved Protector Guardian:

> He wanted something—wanted the thing she always found it so difficult to give him; wanted her to tell him that she loved him. And that, no, she could not do.[40]

Guardians and Rationals often have difficulty speaking their love, Guardians out of their personal modesty, and Rationals out of their desire for intellectual self-control.

---

[39] Virginia Woolf, *To the Lighthouse*, p. 184.
[40] Virginia Woolf, *To the Lighthouse*, p. 184.

And in this moving scene Woolf shows an even more reticent *introverted* Guardian and Rational attempting to find their way back to intimacy without resorting to a single intimate word. Mr. Ramsay's gentle reproof about the stocking (hinting, perhaps, that they might make the trip after all?) is his clumsy Rational way of offering his apology, while Mrs. Ramsay responds not with loving words but with a Guardian's typical offer of service. Since she knows "she never could say what she felt," she wonders instead, "Was there no crumb on his coat? Nothing she could do for him?"

Though neither can command the words of love, their very shyness in each other's presence seems to express the tenderness they feel, and as Mrs. Ramsay turns again and looks at her husband, the pettiness of the evening's animosity falls away, and their long-nurtured habit of affection quietly reaffirms itself:

> And as she looked at him she began to smile, for though she had not said a word, he knew, of course he knew, that she loved him.[41]

Thus, finally, standing on the stable foundation not only of her own personal dignity but also of her marriage, Mrs. Ramsay can offer her husband the interpersonal victory he needs for his own self-esteem, and so resolve their conflict once and for all before they darken the house for the night:

---

[41] Virginia Woolf, *To the Lighthouse*, p. 185.

And smiling she looked out of the window and said (thinking
to herself, Nothing on earth can equal this happiness)—
    "Yes, you were right. It's going to be wet tomorrow. You
won't be able to go.[42]

As a Protector, Mrs. Ramsay cherishes perhaps above all
else the "community of feeling," she finds in her marriage,
"as if the walls of partition had become so thin that
practically (the feeling was one of relief and happiness) it
was all one stream." And on this night, as the stormy
"harvest moon" looks down outside, she and her husband
break through their angry seperateness and flow together
once again.

Despite the wealth of insight *To the Lighthouse* offers us
about the female Protector's internal life, Virginia Woolf's
stream-of-consciousness style is misleading in one way
about Protectors—about all the Guardians for that matter.
Guardians are citizens primarily of the real world, and
spend most of their lives *doing* things, concrete, down-to-
earth things, only occasionally giving themselves up to
anything so abstract as introspection. Virginia Woolf's
Guardian characters, however, seem inordinately abstract,
obsessed with observing their inner lives, scrutinizing those
moments, as Woolf puts it, when "the mind raised itself
from the task at hand." But if we keep in mind the kinds of
things Mrs. Ramsay normally concerns herself with—rules
for her children ("windows should be open, and doors
shut"), services to her guests and her husband ("stamps,

---

[42] Virginia Woolf, *To the Lighthouse*, pp. 185-186.

writing paper, tobacco?"), charities to the poor, knitting, seating arrangements, mealtimes, marriage ceremonies, and so on—then she appears every inch a Protector Guardian, and her consuming introspection on this particular September evening is less a matter of her personal desire for self-knowledge than of Virginia Woolf's own fascination with her character's internal depths. Guardians *have* a vital mental life, of course, and Woolf's remarkable talent is precisely for capturing not only the "odds and ends" and "transactions" of life that daily occupy Mrs. Ramsay, but also those more rare and intricate moments of self-awareness that steal upon a lovely, caring, fifty year old Protector whose life for the most part "had slipped past in one quick doing after another."

*   *   *   *   *

Protectors, then, appear in literature the least aggressive Pygmalions of all the Guardians, preferring to shape their partners through the example of their quiet devotion, their spirit of cooperation, and their patient suffering—and not so much through angry conflict or biting rhetoric. Indeed, my three characters all prefer to withdraw from confrontation rather than to manipulate their relationships: Tony Last leaves for the Amazon, Tess Durbeyfield turns to her stony highway, and Mrs. Ramsay pulls inward to reestablish her dignity. Let me reiterate that, in more severely manipulative relationships, such turning away might be a deliberate means of coercion, the Protectors casting themselves as interpersonal victims, and thus trying to shame their spouses into more caring or responsible behavior. But in most cases, Protectors would simply rather tolerate interpersonal conflict silently, at times tragically, hoping that loyalty and service—maintaining the traditions and rituals of a stable homelife—will let them ride out whatever storm the marriage might be caught in. In loving a Protector, we must be aware that, more than any other type, they will suffer in silence, but that beneath their modest and dutiful exterior can lie years of pent-up irritation and resentment. If we can appreciate Protectors for their dependability and gentle nurturing, and stop taking them for granted or, even worse, taking *advantage* of them, we can save them their suffering and free them to flourish in their safeguarding.

Chapter 3

The
Provider

I have nothing to offer you but ... my honesty for your surety, my ability and industry for your livlihood, and my authority and position for your dignity.

————George Bernard Shaw[1]

While Protectors primarily concern themselves with the safety of the nest, prefering to nurture their spouses and children privately, the more sociable Conservator Guardians, the type Keirsey calls the Providers (Myers's "ESFJ's"), extend their caretaking outside the home and the immediate family. Providers are just as conscientious in their family obligations as Protectors, and are perhaps the most warm-hearted of all the types,[2] but their more gregarious nature makes them more aware of their responsibilities to the community at large, and they seem at times more

---

[1] George Bernard Shaw, *Candida* (Penguin ed., 1969), p. 72.
[2] David Keirsey and Marilyn Bates, *Please Understand Me*, p. 193.

interested in doing their *public* part—on the job, at the club, in church or school volunteer work—than in simply watching over home and hearth. This outer-directedness also requires the Providers to be somewhat more overtly assertive and manipulative in their personal relationships than the Protectors. Though still essentially cooperative with their loved ones, Providers are more conscious of their social status, their standing in the community—having the right job, the right friends, the right possessions—and so they often push harder to make certain their spouses and children behave in a socially acceptable manner, contributing to their position as a solid citizen. Providers are thus the most natural social conformists among the types, and literature frequently satirizes their careful conventionality, quite unfairly disregarding the Providers' unique virtues: their vitality and devotion, their gracious concern for others, and their sincere desire to maintain a stable, respectable community.

George F. Babbitt

In the course of his long career as a novelist, Sinclair Lewis ridiculed virtually every characteristic of the American small-businessman, but in *Babbitt*, perhaps his most successful novel, Lewis combined his satire with a certain admiration for what he usually caricatured as the "Solid Citizen." Indeed, Lewis admitted "I wrote *Babbitt* not out of hatred for him but out of love," and while he laughs openly at a whole range of crass, self-important, backslapping business types in the novel, Lewis observes George F. Babbitt with a surprising sympathy, and in amazing detail. The novel's first seven chapters compass only twenty-four hours in Babbitt's life—a typical business day, "from alarm clock to alarm clock"—and such close analysis reveals quite affectionately the vicissitudes of life and love for the male Provider Guardian.

Babbitt awakens slowly and irritably on an April morning in 1920, vexed into consciousness by the rumble of the milk-truck, the slam of the furnace-man, the whistle and thump of the paper-boy, and the "snap-ah-ah" rattle of a neighbor cranking his Ford. Babbitt is savoring the last moments of a favorite Guardian sexual fantasy, sailing away with a Sensualist Artisan "fairy girl" ("so slim, so white, so eager"), and though he tries clinging to his dream, the suburban neighborhood noises keep calling him back to his life of responsibilities as a prosperous real estate salesman, a virtuous husband and father, and a trustworthy pillar of the community. Of course, Providers respond more agreeably to a high-class call to duty than to such coarse, inconsiderate noise, and so when Babbitt's "nationally advertised" alarm clock finally sounds its stylish cathedral chime, he rouses himself to face the day, "proud of being awakened by such a rich device."

Babbitt is also proud of his Dutch Colonial tract house in Floral Heights, a new residential development in his typically mid-American hometown of Zenith. As he pads down the hall to his "altogether royal" bathroom, he looks out the window at his tidy yard, smiles with satisfaction at its standardized "perfection," and promises himself to replace the cheap corrugated iron garage with an up-to-date wooden frame structure. Providers love to plan home-improvements, always figuring ways to refurbish their nests, and Babbitt's determination to shape up his garage buoys his self-esteem: "He suddenly seemed capable, an official, a man...to get things done."

But the chaos of the bathroom rudely assaults his confidence. The floor is wet, the bath mat is wrinkled (his daughter "eccentrically took baths in the morning"), and the air reeks of "heathen toothpaste...some confounded stinkum stuff," instead of the family's regular brand. Guardians seem to have a talent for finding inconvenience, as if trying to make the world admit just how poorly organized it is, and Babbitt dutifully slips on the mat, bumps against the tub, fumbles with his razor ("Damn—oh—oh—damn it!"), fumes at his wife for hiding his new blades behind the bicarbonate of soda, and finally, finding all the family towels "wet and clammy and vile," he throws caution to the wind and wipes his face on the pansy-embroidered guest-towel.

To a Provider Guardian like Babbitt, the guest-towel is a sacred institution—no one, including his guests, has ever dared lay hands on it—and being driven to such desperate measures both embarrasses and infuriates him. "By golly," Babbitt mutters to himself,

> here they go and use up all the towels, every doggone one of
> 'em, and they use 'em and get 'em all wet and sopping and
> never put out a dry one for me—of course, I'm the goat!—and
> then I want one and—I'm the only person in the doggone
> house that's got the slightest doggone bit of consideration for
> other people and thoughtfulness and consider there may be
> others that may want to use the doggone bathroom after me.[3]

To the Provider, selfishness and thoughtlessness are the two
unforgivable sins, and Babbitt, lecturing to the bathtub,
crossly scolds his family for their disgraceful lack of
consideration, quite "pleased by the vindictiveness" of his
tone.

Dressing for work comes next, and after engaging his wife
Myra (a Conservator Guardian herself) in a "thorough
discussion of all the domestic and social aspects of towels,"
Babbitt begins his morning ritual. The episode that follows
is a wonderful parody of the epic dressing-for-battle scenes
in ancient poems and plays, in which the knight/warrior
heroically straps on his culture's virtues with his armor or
his colors. In this more modern, suburban version, however,
Lewis's dialogue captures all the fuss and bother of two
long-married Conservator Guardians circling each other
verbally, trying to settle on what to wear without either one
actually taking responsibility for the decision:

---

[3] Sinclair Lewis, *Babbitt* (Signet ed., 1950), p. 9. All quotations are
from this edition. Although Edith Wharton, for one, objected to
Lewis's excessive use of slang in Babbitt's speech, Lewis succeeded
amazingly well in capturing the irritable, mildly expletory male-
Guardian diction.

"What do you think, Myra?" He pawed at the clothes hunched on the chair in their bedroom, while she moved about mysteriously adjusting and patting her petticoat and, to his jaundiced eye, never seeming to get on with her dressing. "How about it? Shall I wear the brown suit another day?"

"Well, it looks awfully nice on you."

"I know, but gosh, it needs pressing."

"That's so. Perhaps it does."

"It certainly could stand being pressed, all right."

"Yes, perhaps it wouldn't hurt to be pressed."

"But gee, the coat doesn't need pressing. No sense in having the whole darn suit pressed, when the coat doesn't need it."

"That's so."

"But the pants certainly need it, all right. Look at them— look at those wrinkles—the pants certainly do need pressing."

"That's so. Oh, Georgie, why couldn't you wear the brown coat with blue trousers we were wondering what we'd do with them?"

"Good Lord! Did you ever in all my life know me to wear the coat of one suit and the pants of another? What do you think I am, a busted bookkeeper?"

"Well, why don't you put on the dark gray suit to-day, and stop in at the tailor and leave the brown trousers?"

"Well, they certainly need— Now where the devil is that gray suit?"[4]

Babbitt and Myra's "conference on the brown suit" is a good example of what Keirsey calls the Conservator Guardians' typically role-informative style of communication in their relationships. Note in this instance how Babbitt and Myra offer information about the brown suit ("it looks nice on you"..."but it needs pressing") rather than either one of them taking hold of the decision and directing that he either wear the suit another day or take it to the cleaners.

---

[4] Sinclair Lewis, *Babbitt*, pp. 10-11.

As Conservator Guardians, Babbitt and Myra are more comfortable responding to each other than in telling each other what to do, and thus defining who is in charge of their relationship. Let me point out that Babbitt and Myra are not avoiding or putting off the decision; they both feel the desire for closure that characterizes all the Guardians, but they are simply reluctant to take command. And thus, even late in their conversation, after they have worried the decision almost to death, each resorts to qualified or indirect commands (leading questions such as "why couldn't you?" "what do you think?" or "why don't you?") to offer settlement of the issue as obliquely as possible.[5]

In any event, after Babbitt and Myra have successfully nudged each other to a decision, Babbitt commences his daily dressing routine. First, he pulls on his sleeveless B.V.D. undershirt (a lengthy search had finally turned it up, "malevolently concealed among his clean pajamas"). Next he combs back his thin brown hair, and dons his huge, frameless spectacles, which magically transform him into "the modern business man; one who gave orders to clerks and drove a car and played occasional golf and was scholarly in regard to Salesmanship." And then he proceeds to put on the rest of what Lewis calls his "uniform as a Solid Citizen," from his vest with white piping that suggests a "flavor of law and learning," to his black boots, "good boots, honest boots, standard boots."

---

[5] See *Portraits of Temperament*, pp. 13-14, for Keirsey's general theory of temperamental differences in RoleMessages, and pp. 54-55, for the Conservator Guardians' role-informative style of communication.

But this morning, as the ritual progresses, Babbitt must transfer the contents of his pockets from the brown suit to the gray, and like Tony Last savoring his family collections, Babbitt "was earnest about these objects. They were of eternal importance, like baseball or the Republican party." His pen, pencil, penknife, key ring, watch, and cigar-cutter each has its assigned pocket, and without each faithfully tucked in its place Babbitt admits "he would have felt naked." He also carries a loose-leaf pocket note-book filled with important names and addresses, "prudent memoranda" of things he has forgotten to do, old stamps, and clippings of newspaper editorials that Babbitt passionately agrees with and wants to make sure his friends read. By the way, Keirsey observes that Providers usually gather their "opinions and attitudes" about society and politics from authoritative sources[6]; and Lewis similarly points out that until one of Zenith's newspapers or the Chamber of Commerce bulletin "had spoken" on an issue, Babbitt "found it hard to form an original opinion."

Two oddities add a dash of color to Babbitt's attire, a large, yellowish elk's tooth hanging from his watch-chain, and a loud Booster's Club button pinned to his lapel, and both call attention to an important feature of the Provider's makeup. Providers often meet two of their basic needs, membership and service, by taking an active part in lodges and civic organizations, and clearly Babbitt is a "joiner" in his very essence: "His clubs and associations," Lewis re-

---

[6] David Keirsey and Marilyn Bates, *Please Understand Me*, p. 193.

marks, "were food comfortable to his spirit." Thus the elk's tooth signifies Babbitt's membership in the "Benevolent and Protective Order of Elks," one of a dozen or so secret orders in American business culture that Lewis describes as "characterized by a high degree of heartiness, sound morals, and reverence for the Constitution." In addition, the Booster's Club button proclaims Babbitt's energetic participation in a weekly lunch-club dedicated to "sound business and friendliness among Regular Fellows." Indeed, the Booster's Club philosophy, and very much the Provider's creed, is spelled out on their luncheon place-cards:

> I believe the highest type of Service... is motivated by active adherence and loyalty to that which is the essential principle of Boosterism—Good Citizenship in all its factors and aspects.[7]

Like all the Guardians, Providers are incurably social creatures, and Babbitt's work in these fraternal organizations not only lets him feel "loyal and important," but also allows him to exercise his talent for working with people. His amiability and gift for oratory have lifted him to the rank of "Esteemed Leading Knight" in the Elk's Club, and he has recently been elected vice-president of the Booster's for his good business sense and his "Pep." Unfortunately, all of these honors take their toll, and Babbitt cannot resist a Guardian's rather self-satisfied complaining about how overworked and unappreciated he is. His many "official duties," he boasts wearily to a client,

---

[7] Sinclair Lewis, *Babbitt*, p. 210.

mean "a lot of work and responsibility—and practically no gratitude for it."

Lewis mentions that Babbitt often comes "bouncing and jesting into breakfast," but on this fine spring morning he finishes dressing with more than a little gloom. He moans to Myra that he feels "kind of punk," a condition he immediately blames on her heavy fried foods, and this mention of stomach ailments sets him off on a Provider's favorite discourse, delivered in their typically disconnected, word to the wise style:

> I tell you, when a fellow gets past forty he has to look after his digestion. There's a lot of fellows that don't take proper care of themselves. I tell you a man's a fool or his doctor— I mean, his own doctor. Folks don't give enough attention to this matter of dieting. Now I think— Course a man ought to have a good meal after the day's work, but it would be a good thing for both of us if we took lighter lunches.[8]

The subject of their aches and pains has a particular fascination for all the Guardians,[9] and as Babbitt hunts for his pocket-change he pursues his dyspeptic theme, turning from one complaint to the next, and hitting eventually on a familiar Guardian remedy:

> But I certainly do feel out of sorts this morning. Funny, got a pain down here on the left side—but no, that wouldn't be

---

[8] Sinclair Lewis, *Babbitt*, p. 12.

[9] Keirsey identifies the Monitor Guardians as the full-blown Hypochondriac Depressives (*Portraits of Temperament*, p. 51), but he points out that the Conservator Guardians are also "prone to complain of fears for their health" (*Portraits of Temperament*, p. 62).

appendicitis would it? Last night...I felt a sharp pain in my
stomach, too. Right here it was—kind of a sharp shooting
pain. I— Where'd that dime go to? Why don't you serve more
prunes at breakfast? Of course I eat an apple every evening—
an apple a day keeps the doctor away—but still, you ought to
have more prunes, and not all these fancy doodads.[10]

Although worries with indigestion and constipation seem to
preoccupy the Guardians,[11] in truth almost any disorder—
back, shoulder, teeth, a quick cold or a chronic condition—
is fair game for their anxiety, and is faithfully and gravely
complained of to their family members. Of course, we all
enjoy extra sympathy when we are mildly out of sorts. But
Provider Guardians like Babbitt, normally so generous with
their concern for others, and so weighed down with their
own responsibilities, seem especially eager to share their
infirmities with their loved ones, as if needing to

---

[10] Sinclair Lewis, *Babbitt*, p. 13.

[11] Franz Alexander, the early authority on psychsomatic disease,
clearly connects gastro-intestinal difficulties with the typical
Guardian style of life. First, Alexander describes the behavior of the
Guardians with uncanny accuracy: "Collecting different objects,
ordering and classifying them (as a sign of the mastery of them),
also the fear of losing something, the rejection of the obligation to
give something, the impulse to hide and protect things from being
taken away or from deterioration." And then he reveals their
particular psychosomatic disposition: "all of these may find
expression in retentive physiological innervations. The best known
of these is constipation." As for Babbitt's nagging stomach pains,
Alexander also points out that Guardians are apt to compensate for
their "strong receptive-dependent" temperament "by assuming
responsibilities and by concentrated efforts in work," and end up
suffering from "gastric neurosis or peptic ulcer." See Alexander's
article, "The Logic of Emotions and Its Dynamic Background,"
International Journal of Psychoanalysis, 16:1935, pp. 405, 407.

demonstrate how difficult and disabling their life has been before they feel properly appreciated.

Babbitt soon makes it down to breakfast, but his children's difficulties only add to his indigestion. His twenty-two year old daughter Verona (a romantic young Idealist) has a "nice" job as a filing-clerk, with prospects of becoming a private secretary, but she feels spiritually unfulfilled and greets Babbitt at breakfast with the news that she wants to quit her job and do charity work in a settlement-house. Babbitt is appalled at the thought of his daughter wasting her "expensive college education" on the poor, and he tries to clear her head with a stiff dose of his Conservator's shoulder-to-the-wheel political philosophy:

> Now you look here! The first thing you got to understand is that all this... settlement-work and recreation is nothing in God's world but the entering wedge of socialism. The sooner a man learns he isn't going to be coddled, and he needn't expect a lot of free grub and, uh, all these free classes and flipflop and doodads for his kids unless he earns 'em, why, the sooner he'll get on the job and produce—produce—produce! That's what the country needs, and not all this fancy stuff that just enfeebles the will-power of the working man and gives his kids a lot of notions above their class.[12]

Babbitt's seventeen year old son Ted (Theodore Roosevelt Babbitt, a rough and ready Artisan like his namesake) interrupts these serious matters by asking to use the family car after dinner, and in the ensuing argument claims that,

---

[12] Sinclair Lewis, *Babbitt*, p. 17.

really, to fit in with his upper class high school fraternity crowd he needs a car of his own. The idea that his own son is harboring "fancy notions" above his class galls Babbitt's earnest self-reliance, and his admonishing tone quickly turns to sarcasm:

> That pretty nearly takes the cake! A boy that can't pass his Latin examinations, like any other boy ought to, and he expects me to give him a motorcar, and I suppose a chauffeur, and an aeroplane maybe, as a reward for the hard work he puts in going to the movies.[13]

Babbitt is gentler with ten year old Katherine (another Artisan, it appears, and easily Daddy's favorite), waiting until she has gone upstairs to complain of her fondness for sweets. "Say," he reproaches Myra, "don't let Tinka go and eat any more of that poison nut-fudge. For Heaven's sake, try to keep her from ruining her digestion."

In his concern for his wife and children's behavior, certainly, Babbitt is a dedicated Pygmalion. If they would all just eat more sensibly, or "tend to business instead of fooling and fussing," or go to school and "make good"—all of which are Guardian disciplines that Babbitt staunchly believes in—then they would all be happier, and they would leave off the constant bickering and "jabbering" that accosts him even at the breakfast table. Of course, Babbitt is largely unaware of his own Pygmalion role in the family hostilities, what Lewis calls "the greatest of the Great Wars, which is

---

[13] Sinclair Lewis, *Babbitt*, p. 19.

the family war." With an irony that clearly escapes him, Babbitt himself sets much of the carping tone for the family, even though his purpose is quite the opposite: he picks at his wife and children in order to create more harmonious family relations—he fusses at them to stop their fussing. As I have said, Conservator Guardians are caring, nurturing types at heart, and Babbitt sculpts away at his family not ruthlessly nor punitively, but with the best of intentions, getting after them more out of fondness than severity. "He really disliked being a family tyrant," Lewis discloses, "and his nagging was as meaningless as it was frequent."

The children off to work and school, Babbitt finishes his breakfast over the morning paper, recounting grimly to Myra all the natural and political disasters in the headlines. But he stops and reads aloud a long item in the society column that describes a lavish dinner party at the McKelvey mansion, one of the newest and most luxurious houses in Zenith. As a prosperous middle class Provider, Babbitt has a curiously ambivalent attitude toward such nuveau riche socialites—"plutes," as he calls them. In the first place, Babbitt resents the McKelveys' snobbish "sassiety stunts" and he bitterly disparages the whole "gang of highbinders," with all their Artisan "booze-hoisting" and "highbrow talk." Like all the Guardians, Babbitt is highly conscious of class distinctions, but he believes the only proper class for him and his like is "the gentleman class—the class that are just as red-blooded as the Common People but still have power and personality." To Babbitt, building grand houses and throwing expensive parties is wasteful and pretentious, just showing off your riches to feel socially superior. Babbitt is proud of having sacrificed for his own solid success, and he's not about to throw away his hard-earned money on senseless ostentation. He even brags to Myra, showing his true Guardian measure of men,

> I'll bet I make a whole lot more money than some of those tin-horns that spend all they got on dress-suits and haven't got a decent suit of underwear to their name![14]

But at the same time that Babbitt condemns the McKelveys, he also deeply covets their social position and their pretensions of aristocracy. The McKelveys are leaders of the "Smart Set" in Zenith, an exclusive and wealthy country-club crowd that Babbitt secretly aspires to, and even plots to join. Indeed, Babbitt goes all out later in the novel and invites the McKelveys to a formal champagne dinner at his home in Floral Heights (he loves performing his "duty as a host"), and then he checks in the society column for weeks afterwards, looking for mention of the affair, or for rumors of a return invitation.

Of course, while Babbitt condemns and flatters the Smart Set, he holds the most unequivocal—even hallowed—regard for a few of the city's oldest families. If "Babbitt was envious...of the McKelveys," Lewis tells us,

---

[14] Sinclair Lewis, *Babbitt*, p. 22.

before William Washington Eathorne [a banker, and heir of a
Founding Family] he was reverent. Mr. Eathorne had nothing
to do with the Smart Set. He was above it.... In his presence
Babbitt breathed quickly and felt young.[15]

As Keirsey points out, the Guardians characteristically
esteem "aristocrats, plutocrats, and persons of high
status,"[16] but let me add that Guardians reserve their whole-
hearted deference for truly noble blood, visiting European
royalty, for instance, or for the dignity and high-breeding of
founding fathers. For first-generation social climbers like
the McKelveys, however, Babbitt maintains a more
hypocritical attitude: he gossips cruelly about them with
Myra, but in public he conspicuously courts their favor.

Finishing his coffee, Babbitt brushes Myra with a kiss and
heads for the garage to begin the daily adventure of getting
to the office. Starting his car is often a nasty struggle for
Babbitt, and as usual, with his Guardian pessimism, "This
morning he was darkly prepared to find something wrong,
and felt belittled when the mixture exploded sweet and
strong." At times, Guardians seem to take pride in their
difficulties, as if they believe that life beleaguers only the
most worthy, and when Babbitt backs out of the garage
uneventfully, without even scraping the door-jamb, Lewis
admits "he was confused."

Driving through the precise streets of Floral Heights,
Babbitt loses more and more of his "dawn depression," and

---

[15] Sinclair Lewis, *Babbitt*, p. 169.
[16] David Keirsey, *Portraits of Temperament*, p. 47; see also p. 58.

when he pulls off the parkway for gas he decides to live it up and fill the tank. For Babbitt, getting gasoline is more than a disagreeable chore; it is a ceremony of social stability and personal service. Providers build their lives on comforting routines, often giving their loyalty to a "regular" service station, or market, or barber-shop, and so on; and thus, as Babbitt pulls up to the well-known red pump, and admires the garage's trim, well-stocked display window, Lewis observes that "the familiarity of the rite fortified him." Providers also love to be personally recognized and appreciated by clerks and attendants—being a *regular* customer confers a certain status—and, indeed, Babbitt

> was flattered by the friendliness with which Sylvester Moon, dirtiest and most skilled of motor mechanics, came out to serve him. "Mornin', Mr. Babbitt," said Moon, and Babbitt felt himself a person of importance, one whose name even busy garagemen remembered.[17]

As the gallons click off on the new-fangled automatic dial, Babbitt and Moon talk over presidential politics, agreeing that what this country needs is "a good, sound business administration"; and as Babbitt is paying the bill, Moon compliments him on how well he takes care of his car, to which Babbitt humbly responds, "Well, I do try and have some sense about it." Well-satisfied with the entire interaction—filled with good-feeling about his community as well as with gasoline—Babbitt tips Moon generously, and drives off in what Lewis describes as "an ecstasy of honest self-appreciation."

---

[17] Sinclair Lewis, *Babbitt*, p. 26.

Heading back onto the parkway, Babbitt offers a lift to a waiting trolley commuter, not so much out of bleeding heart "generosity," as he assures the man, but out of his sense of "duty to share the good things of this world with his neighbors." Unlike the Artisans, for whom generosity is a natural, spontaneous gesture, Provider Guardians see any type of offering as an act of charity, and so their generosity, though well-meant, is often forced and clumsy. Still, Providers are friendly and talkative types, devotedly striking up conversations even with perfect strangers, and as Babbitt proceeds on his customary route downtown, he nearly talks the poor man's ear off, only releasing this "victim of benevolence," as Lewis calls him, when he pulls up in front of his office building.

Babbitt enters his clean, reputable real estate office still a little cranky, but with a growing confidence in his gifts as a Provider, in "his own faith that he was going to make sales." Babbitt owns the Babbitt-Thompson Realty Company with his father-in-law, Henry Thompson, a Promoter Artisan (an "ESTP") wheeler-dealer who operates somewhat suspiciously behind the scenes, negotiating the big development deals. Babbitt's value to the firm is quite different from old Henry's, and Lewis's statement of the contrast is wonderfully succinct:

> Babbitt's virtues as a real-estate broker... were steadiness and diligence. He was conventionally honest, he kept his records

of buyers and sellers complete, he had experience with leases and titles and an excellent memory for prices.[18]

Babbitt thus manages the company's honest, dependable side; as a Provider he presents himself as "servant of society... finding homes for families," a Good Fellow whose "duty and privilege" it is to know everything about his community, as well as about "a thing called Ethics," and who earns his clients' trust by his "slow cautiousness." This is not to say that Babbitt is "unreasonably honest," mind you. Guardians know the value of a dollar better than any other temperament, and Lewis admits that Babbitt was not so "impractical [as to] refuse to take twice the price of a house" if the buyer was willing to pay. No matter how essentially ethical they are, when money is changing hands Providers often undergo an amazing transformation. Their characteristic concern for others becomes suddenly less forthcoming, and for business purposes they can assume an attitude of "let the buyer beware." Providers may begin to feel guilty if they take too much advantage of others, but they harbor few illusions about human greed, and are fully capable of competing effectively in the market-place. Indeed, Babbitt justifies his slightly embellished "selling-spiels" with his deep-seated Guardian belief in the corruption of mankind. "And then most folks are so darn crooked themselves," he is convinced, "that they expect a fellow to do a little lying." However, in all fairness, Babbitt is rather tame and conventional even in his sharper

---

[18] Sinclair Lewis, *Babbitt*, p. 37.

practices. "He followed the custom of his clan," Lewis explains, "and cheated only as it was sanctified by precedent."

Babbitt's morning tasks at the office are also quite tame. He congratulates himself on his expensive water-cooler, and composes a cemetary plot rental advertisement ("When the last sad rites of bereavement are over, do you know for certain that you have done your best for the Departed?"). He dictates a form-letter "diligently imitative of the best literary models," and he makes his monthly vow to quit smoking in perfect Provider fashion:

> He went through with it like the solid citizen he was: he admitted the evils of tobacco, courageously made resolves, laid out plans to check the vice, tapered off his allowance of cigars, and expounded the pleasures of virtuousness to every one he met. He did everything, in fact, except stop smoking.[19]

But despite his morning's diligence, Babbitt finds himself badly bored and aggravated by all this "sitting and thinking instead of bustling around and making noise and really doing something." Guardians and Artisans may show many opposite characteristics, but they are very much alike in this one fundamental way: both temperaments are far happier *doing* things than *thinking* about things. Theirs is primarily a concrete reality, not an abstract one, although, of course, what they do and how they do it is widely different.

A ticklish, private sales conference finally gives Babbitt something to *do*, and relieves some of his anxiety; but when

---

[19] Sinclair Lewis, *Babbitt*, pp. 35-36.

he lapses into a confusing sexual fantasy about his
secretary, he is frustrated all the more. Babbitt woke up this
morning dreaming once again of his sensuous "fairy girl,"
and now, as he watches his young secretary Miss McGoun
finish her dictation, he "imagined their eyes meeting with
terrifying recognition; imagined touching her lips with
frightened reverence." Restrained as they are by their
sincere belief in propriety and family duty, Guardian men
tend to conjure up a rather hungry—and a rather guilty—
sexual fantasy life, and Lewis tells us that in Babbitt's
"twenty-three years of married life he had peered uneasily
at every graceful ankle, every soft shoulder." Let me
emphasize that Babbitt dreams of love very much in male-
Guardian style, not to be confused with an Idealist's more
soulful (and at times more dissipated) longings. To be sure,
Babbitt's view of women is at once more down-to-earth and
more strictly organized, as Lewis explains:

> Babbitt was not an analyst of women, except as to their tastes
> in Furnished Houses to Rent. He divided them into Real
> Ladies, Working Women, Old Cranks, and Fly Chickens. He
> mooned over their charms but was of opinion that all of them
> (save the women of his own family) were "different" and
> "mysterious."[20]

Babbitt has little insight into the female, and, unlike the
more intimate and empathic Idealist, he keeps from
thinking about women as individuals by fitting them neatly
into a handful of pre-determined social or sexual categories.

---

[20] Sinclair Lewis, *Babbitt*, p. 104.

Thus, in an unconscious, internal Pygmalion project, Babbitt shapes the women around him into more easily comprehensible caricatures, defining them sexually in one of two ways: either as respectable or erotic, as admirable or alluring—either as a comfortable wife to be served faithfully, or as a "mysterious" mistress to be yearned for secretly.

Babbitt's attitude toward his wife Myra certainly follows this line, and explains a great deal about his wandering eye. Even when they were dating, Babbitt placed Myra into a category that was essentially asexual. He thought of her as "a Nice Girl—one didn't kiss her, one didn't 'think of her that way at all' unless one was going to marry her." Myra, after some months of chaste but dependable companionship, assumed that she had satisfied all the rules of courtship and had become engaged to her "young man." On his side, Babbitt was sure he felt no physical passion for this "tender woman thing," but as a conscientious Provider he "could not hurt her, could not abuse her trust." And so these two innocent Conservator Guardians dutifully married, overcame their sexual inhibitions for a time—and then settled into "mature family life," a marriage-style each of them found innately more comfortable than romantic "young love." Keirsey argues that often in Guardian-Guardian marriages, "Sex...is something one does at night, in the bedroom, as quietly as possible, and, after some years of marriage, perhaps as seldom as possible."[21] And Lewis

---

[21] David Keirsey and Marilyn Bates, *Please Understand Me*, p. 83.

describes the same withering process in Babbitt and Myra's relationship:

> She made him what is known as a Good Wife. She was loyal, industrious, and at rare times merry. She passed from a feeble disgust at their closer relations into what promised to be ardent affection, but it drooped into bored routine.[22]

Now, some twenty years later, although Babbitt is content to think of himself as an "extremely married and unromantic" Provider Guardian, he timidly pursues what he regards as a shameful fantasy life. He dreams at night of sensual escape, he glances furtively at his secretary, he searches all of his friends' wives for signs of loneliness, he even imagines daring liasons with shop-girls and manicurists—"in thought he had treasured them [all]," Lewis confesses, but adds that Babbitt is "ashamed of his discontentment," and "not once had he hazarded respectability by adventuring."

A lunch-date with his friend Paul Reisling is an adventure more agreeable to Babbitt's conscience, and as he drives across town to the Zenith Athletic Club he re-directs his dreams of erotic conquest into his almost daily mental audit of his economic success. "Let's see," he quickly calculates,

> I ought to pull out eight thousand net this year, and save fifteen hundred of that....Let's see: six hundred and forty clear last month, and twelve times six-forty makes—makes— let see...anyway, I'll make eight thousand—gee now, that's not so bad; mighty few fellows pulling down eight thousand

---

[22] Sinclair Lewis, *Babbitt*, p. 76.

dollars a year... bet there isn't more than five fer cent. of the people in the whole United States that make more than Uncle George does, by golly! Right up at the top of the heap![23]

Keirsey points out, however, that for Providers "the economic problem is never completely solved,"[24] and, indeed, in the midst of his self-satisfaction Babbitt remembers to worry about the various drains on his finances. "But," he cautions himself, "Way expenses are— Family wasting gasoline, and always dressed like millionaires, and sending that eighty a month to Mother — And all these stenographers and salesmen gouging me for every cent they can get...." No matter how well-off they might become, Guardians are never fully secure in their prosperity; their natural assumption is that economic disaster is just around the corner, and indeed, as Babbitt does "his old familiar sums" in the car, he feels all the ambivalence of a well-to-do but pessimistic Provider. "The effect of his scientific budget-planning," Lewis says, "was that he felt at once triumphantly wealthy and perilously poor."

Babbitt's lunch starts off amiably enough. He is greeted at the club by the "Roughnecks," a group of his Elk's and Booster's cronies, and they all trade friendly insults about each other's shady business deals, their henpecked marriages, their poker parties, and so on. Providers rarely let their guard down at home or at the office—life is always serious business—so that "lunch out with the boys," with all the good-natured teasing and ribbing, can be a welcome

---

[23] Sinclair Lewis, *Babbitt*, p. 46.
[24] David Keirsey, *Portraits of Temperament*, p. 56.

break from their careful routine, and Babbitt plays what
Lewis calls the "blaring Good Fellow, the Josher and
Regular Guy" with the best of them.

However, when he and Paul are seated alone, the mood
turns more somber, and Lewis begins to express some of
his well-known criticism of Babbitt's conservative
Guardian way of life. Paul is an outsider in Babbitt's
commercial world; he is an Instrumentalist Artisan (an
"ISTP") who gave up his ambition to be a violinist, and
who now finds himself trapped in both a dull sales career
and a hateful, violent marriage. Babbitt and Paul often talk
openly, more as brothers than as friends, and today Babbitt
shares some of his morning's strange restlessness, certain
that "old Paulski" will understand:

> here I've pretty much done all the things I ought to; supported
> my family, and got a good house and a six-cylinder car, and
> built up a nice little business, and... I belong to the church, and
> play enough golf to keep in trim, and I only associate with
> good decent fellows. And yet, even so, I don't know that I'm
> entirely satisfied.[25]

Babbitt's confession is rather idle, just a Provider's vague
grumblings, but it touches Paul powerfully, and he takes up
the implied criticism of America's business culture with
much of Lewis's own passion. Paul cynically attacks his

---

[25] Sinclair Lewis, *Babbitt*, p. 52. Babbitt's exhausting attempt to fulfill
all possible Provider roles for his family sounds very much as if he
is playing a masculine form of the interpersonal game that Eric
Berne calls "Harried." See Eric Berne, *Games People Play*
(Ballantine ed., 1964), pp. 101-104.

own life and marriage, and contends further that two-thirds of American businessmen, including Babbitt, "hate the whole peppy, boosting, go-ahead game, and they're bored by their wives and think their families are fools." Babbitt grows uneasy, and then alarmed, at this wild "Bolsheviki" talk; Providers might complain about how tired they are, but they are essentially hard-working individuals, and Babbitt finally interrupts Paul to set the record straight:

> Babbitt snorted. "What do you expect? Think we were sent into the world to have a soft time and—what is it?—'float on flowery beds of ease'? Think Man was just made up to be happy?"

Paul responds like a true Artisan:

> Why not? Though I've never discovered anybody that knew what the deuce Man really was made for!

And now quite appalled, Babbitt tries to settle the issue by insisting on the Provider's God-fearing belief in duty, though he tries not to sound too religious in front of Paul:

> Well we know—not just in the Bible alone, but it stands to reason—a man who doesn't buckle down and do his duty, even if it does bore him sometimes, is nothing but a—well, he's simply a weakling.[26]

In spite of their vehemence, Paul and Babbitt value their friendship much more than their disagreement, and they both back down awkwardly, Paul admitting he just wants to "make life more fun," and Babbitt softening his "defense of duty and Christian patience." They even agree that a

---

[26] Sinclair Lewis, *Babbitt*, p. 55.

camping holiday in Maine without the wives would do
them both a world of good—just "one mild bat [to the] old
pillar of monogamy," as Paul puts it—and Babbitt drives
back to his office glowing with the prospect of such an
audacious adventure.

After lunch, Babbitt busies himself with "an afternoon of
not unagreeable details," driving a customer around town,
answering telephone calls, and signing his morning's
letters. While this stretch of purposeful activity brings
Babbitt welcome satisfaction, he does have to face one
annoying task: he must confront one of his salesmen and
argue him out of a much-needed raise in pay. Like most
Providers, Babbitt would rather avoid such antagonism in
his working relationships. "This was a part of office routine
which he feared," Lewis admits, adding that the good-
natured Babbitt "liked people so much, he so much wanted
them to like him, that he could not bear insulting them."
Conservator Guardians in general prefer respect and
cooperation in the workplace, as well as in the family, and
as we have seen they can become quite grouchy trying to
maintain cordial relations. But Lewis understands full well
the real reason why Babbitt gathers his courage and does
what he calls the "Unpleasant duty" of hauling his young
salesman over the coals. Lewis comments again that
Babbitt "liked to like the people about him; he was
dismayed when they did not like him"; but he also explains
that, "when they attacked the sacred purse strings…he was
frightened into fury."

Unfortunately, contention and dismay seem to follow Babbitt home from the office. At dinner, he casually mentions that perhaps it's time for a new car, and the family erupts into pleas for a modern, stylish, and much more expensive closed sedan. Babbitt holds the line ("Don't believe in this business of going and spending a whole lot of money to show off"), and he announces, partly out of spite and under howls of protest, that he thinks he'll drive his convertible another year. Then after dinner, while Babbitt performs his solemn nightly ritual of reading the editorials and the comic strips, young Ted interrupts him with a plan to skip college and take correspondence-courses—no more of this useless high school Latin and Shakespeare, Ted explains, but "the real stuff," like boxing, and music, and photography, and short-story writing. Babbitt agrees that education should be brought up-to-date—"Be a good deal better if you took Business English"—but in the mean time Babbitt insists the tried-and-true subjects are the most worthwhile. "Trouble with you, Ted," he counsels, "is you always want to do something different. If you're going to law-school...you'll want to lay in all the English and Latin you can get." Ted begs his father to *suppose* a more exciting (and Artisan) kind of curriculum, but Babbitt finally and angrily closes the discussion:

> But what's the use of a lot of supposing? Supposing never gets you anywhere. No sense supposing when there's a lot of real facts to take into considera....I don't intend to suppose anything of the kind!"[27]

---

[27] Sinclair Lewis, *Babbitt*, pp. 69-70.

All of this arguing and imagining only ends up souring Babbitt's stomach, and so on the way upstairs to bed, he picks up an apple to soothe his system, and he resumes his familiar Pygmalion project as well, hoping to boost his self-esteem with a quick, hit-and-run victory over his wife:

> "An apple a day keeps the doctor away," he enlightened Mrs. Babbitt, for quite the first time in fourteen hours.
> "That's so."
> "An apple is Nature's best regulator."
> "Yes, it———"
> "Trouble with women is, they never have sense enough to form regular habits."
> "Well, I———"
> "Always nibbling and eating between meals.... If it wasn't for me watching out and keeping an eye on our diet——— I'm the only member of this family that appreciates the value of oatmeal for breakfast."[28]

The Provider's concern with maintaining "regular habits" extends to all facets of life, not the least of which is Babbitt's routine at the end of a busy day: his "rites of preparing for bed," as Lewis observes, "were elaborate and unchanging." First, he meticulously closes down the house:

> he locked doors and tried windows and set the heat regulator... [but so] absent-minded was he that he could not remember which window-catches he had inspected, and through the darkness, fumbling at unseen perilous chairs, he crept back to try them all over again.[29]

Next, he thriftily prepares himself for the morning. He decides if his shirt is "clean enough for another day," then

---

[28] Sinclair Lewis, *Babbitt*, pp. 78-79.
[29] Sinclair Lewis, *Babbitt*, p. 79.

takes a deliberate, sensible bath ("He soaped himself, and rinsed himself, and austerely rubbed himself")— although, to be fair, he does indulge his one "luxurious custom" and shaves while lounging in the steaming tub. Finally, after toweling off in his "grave and unbending" way, he readies his private sleeping-porch:

> The blankets had to be tucked in at the foot of his cot....The rag rug was adjusted so that his bare feet would strike it when he arose in the morning. The alarm clock was wound. The hot-water bottle was filled and placed precisely two feet from the bottom of the cot.[30]

Babbitt climbs under the covers, calls "Gnight!" to Myra in the bedroom, and when his "Bohemian" Artisan neighbor rolls in late and annoys him with the cheerful noise of putting up his car, Babbitt stews in his cot ("Why the devil can't some people never get to bed at a reasonable hour?"), until a more respectful silence settles over the neighborhood, and then he falls asleep.

Admittedly, these first seven chapters of *Babbitt* have little plot to them, and almost no exciting action. Babbitt's day is made up of what Lewis aptly identifies as "details of precedence," "scrupulous rituals," and "veiled rebellions," and though in the rest of the novel Babbitt throws off some of his cautiousness and nervously acts on some of his (or perhaps Lewis's) more Artisan impulses, the story never becomes much more than a series of brilliant observations

---

[30] Sinclair Lewis, *Babbitt*, p. 81.

of a typical "Solid Citizen" in all his strengths and weaknesses. But as such, as a faithful, almost sociological record of the Provider Guardian, whom Lewis refers to as the "supporter of the hearthstone which is the basic foundation of our civilization," *Babbitt* is a remarkable achievement, as fascinating in its own way as the most dramatic fiction.

Mrs. Bennet

Whereas George F. Babbitt captures nearly all sides of the male Provider Guardian, the female Provider is considerably more difficult to bring to life in a single character. Since women in our culture have traditionally been less involved than men in breadwinning, they have usually found themselves taking less prominent roles in novels and plays about the struggle for social or financial success. The male Provider might take center stage in certain fictions, shouldering his way in the masculine world of commerce, but the female more commonly acts out her Provider's nature behind the scenes, managing the household, hostessing parties, giving her time to club or church or charity—attending to the social life of her family and her community, and receiving very little appreciation for her efforts. To be sure, literature frequently regards the female Provider's social skills as somewhat frivolous in comparison with the male's. The female Provider is often disparaged in literature as "the perfect hostess," the "club woman," or the "society matron," making it quite difficult to find a sympathetic portrait of her, even among the accurately drawn supporting characters. In any event, to do justice to this vivacious, conscientious type, I want to look at a woman who, although a minor character, nevertheless dominates the beginning of one of the best-loved stories in all of literature—Mrs. Bennet, the irrepressible mother in Jane Austen's novel, *Pride and Prejudice.*

Mrs. Bennet lives quite comfortably with her husband and five grown up daughters in Meryton, a peaceful neighborhood in Hertfordshire, north of London. Mr. and Mrs. Bennet are late-eighteenth century landed gentry, which means they are people of good—but not noble—breeding, living on a respectable inheritance (two thousand pounds a year), and on a well-ordered family estate named, significantly, "Longbourn." As a settled, well-to-do wife and mother, Mrs. Bennet would seem happily free from a Provider's usual anxieties; still, her nature is to *provide* for her family, and Jane Austen plagues her with three exasperating problems that give ample scope to her temperament.

First, Mrs. Bennet has her five daughters for whom she must find suitable husbands, which to her very simply means *wealthy* husbands. Second, according to an entailment in the Bennet family will, Longbourn and all its belongings must pass on Mr. Bennet's death to the nearest *male* heir in the family, which means that (with no sons of her own to inherit the estate) Mrs. Bennet must eventually suffer the indignity of being turned out of her own home.

And third, Mr. Bennet is a Definer Rational (an "INTP") who rarely leaves his library, and who takes little more than an amused, sardonic interest in his family's social and economic tribulations. Thus, Mrs. Bennet directs much of her energy in the novel (and Jane Austen much of her irony) toward providing for her daughters and for herself, or coercing an unresponsive Mr. Bennet into doing his family duty and lending a hand. Warm-hearted, effusive, concerned for her daughters' happiness, but also rather gossipy and manipulative and worried for her own status in the community, Mrs. Bennet bustles through the first third of *Pride and Prejudice* with all the officious resolve of a Provider Guardian in full pursuit of a Pygmalion project.

As *Pride and Prejudice* begins, Mrs. Bennet has already heard her call to action. The news has lately reached her that a wealthy young bachelor—a Mr. Bingley—has taken a house in the neighborhood, and Jane Austen's famous opening sentence gently teases the good lady's instinctively economic view of human relationships. "It is a truth universally acknowledged," Austen roundly observes, as if summarizing Mrs. Bennet's conventional attitude, "that a single man in possession of a good fortune, must be in want of a wife." The English landed gentry were an idle class, with no productive or saleable skills; they lived in an inflexible social hierarchy, on fixed, inherited incomes, and the only honorable way for a young woman to secure her future was through a lucrative marriage. Thus Mrs. Bennet, and all the other Provider mothers in the neighborhood, look upon such an eligible young man as literally a stroke of good "fortune." Sight unseen, the unsuspecting Mr. Bingley "is considered as the rightful property of some one or other of their daughters," and indeed, as soon as the gossip circulates that such a matrimonial godsend is to arrive at Netherfield Park in his coach and four by Michaelmas, Mrs. Bennet gathers her wits about her and determines to secure him and his money for her oldest daughter Jane.

Let me stress again at the outset that Mrs. Bennet's meddling is appropriate conduct for a conscientious mother of her time and class, and of her temperament. It is not the flamboyant scheming of a Performer Artisan such as Dolly Levi in Thornton Wilder's *The Matchmaker*; nor is it the shrewd brokering of an Inspector Guardian such as Lady Bracknell in Oscar Wilde's *The Importance of Being Earnest*. Mrs. Bennet is a heartfelt Provider Guardian who very much wants to see her daughters *happily* married, but who simply defines that happiness in terms of wealth and social status. "If I can but see one of my daughter's happily settled at Netherfield," she confides quite sincerely to her husband, "and all the others equally well married, I shall have nothing to wish for."

Mrs. Bennet's first ambition seems well within her grasp. She has full confidence in her eldest daughter Jane's charms, as well as in her own talent for social maneuvering. The only possible difficulty in landing Mr. Bingley, she fears, might be her unsociable and uncooperative husband. In eighteenth century England, the *father* was responsible for making the acquaintance of young bachelors, and thus Mrs. Bennet must somehow motivate her husband to call on Mr. Bingley as quickly as possible, so that she and the girls may be properly and expeditiously introduced. Fortunately for her children, Mrs. Bennet takes her role as Provider quite seriously, for her husband has disdainfully abdicated any responsibility for his daughters' future, and thinks of them all (except one, Elizabeth) as "silly" and bothersome girls. But unfortunately for her marriage, Mrs. Bennet's Pygmalion project to make her husband "care" about his family responsibilities—to overcome his Rational contempt for social ritual and visit Mr. Bingley—quickly sets off a bristling Guardian-Rational duel of words, one more round in what seems to be a familiar struggle for power in their relationship.

Catching her husband outside his library, Mrs. Bennet approaches him cheerfully—though cautiously—trying not to provoke his scorn, but barely able to hide her relish:

> "My dear Mr. Bennet," said his lady to him one day, "have you heard that Netherfield Park is let at last?"
> Mr. Bennet replied that he had not.
> "But it is," returned she; "for Mrs. Long has just been here and she told me all about it."
> Mr. Bennet made no answer.[31]

In Definer Rational style, Mr. Bennet listens with circumspection, fully aware that his wife wants something from him, but unwilling to follow her lead and

---

[31] Jane Austen, *Pride and Prejudice* (Riverside ed., 1956), p. 1. All quotations are from this edition. The conversation that follows takes place on the first three pages of the novel.

acknowledge her implications—which immediately irritates Mrs. Bennet to a more urgent appeal:

> "Do not you want to know who has taken it?" cried his wife impatiently.

Like the Provider Guardians, Definer Rationals are role-informative types in Keirsey's view,[32] naturally prefering to give information in their conversations, and notice that both Mr. and Mrs. Bennet avoid any explicit directives that would clearly define who is giving commands in the relationship. Even Mrs. Bennet's second question ostensibly elicits information: "Do not you want to know?" But notice also that the negative stress of the question ("Do *not* you"), as well as the agitation in her voice, holds an implicit message and a hidden command: that of course he *should* want to know about this new neighbor, that there would be something wrong with him if he did *not*—and that if he knows what's good for him, he will stop stalling and show some interest in this new tenant.[33]

Mr. Bennet now turns to his wife's question, not to give her the satisfaction of an answer, of course, but merely to point out the manipulative and hypocritical nature of her communication:

---

[32] David Keirsey, *Portraits of Temperament*, p. 76.

[33] Mrs. Bennet's question inadvertently turns the conversation from one primarily of digital communication (communication about things—Bingley, Netherfield, etc.) to one of increasingly abstract analogical communication (communication about the relationship—or who is defining the roles in the marriage). See Watzlawick, Beavin and Jackson, *Pragmatics of Human Communication*.

You want to tell me, and I have no objection to hearing it.

Definer Rationals are the most consistently role-informative of all the types, and Mr. Bennet responds again with virtually neutral information, refusing to obey his wife's implicit directive, and thus denying her control of the relationship. However, this time, and in Rational style, he one-ups her question by moving to a different level of communication. Rationals are uncommonly skillful at foiling Pygmalion projects; they have a formidable ability of engaging in a conversation and at the same time perching themselves above that conversation, observing the structure and the consistency of the arguments, often trying to hold their partners to the point, or commenting on their coercive messages. In this case, instead of playing into his wife's hands and continuing on her level, thrusting and parrying over the new tenant at Netherfield, Mr. Bennet steps above the conversation and comments on the coercive *character* of her communication, identifying the real intention of her question.[34] "*You* want to tell me," he corrects her, and then he asserts his autonomy in the relationship by informing her that he has no objection to listening to her.

Jane Austen (quite probably a Rational herself) seems intent on making fun of Mrs. Bennet, and thus shows her almost entirely missing Mr. Bennet's subtle victory. Her husband's

---

[34] In communication theory, Mr. Bennet's shift is a rather sophisticated one into metacommunication (or communication *about* communication). See Ruesch and Bateson, *Communication: The Social Matrix of Psychiatry.*

mere lack of objection "was invitation enough" for her, Austen observes, and the good lady proceeds breathlessly to rattle off all the latest gossip about Mr. Bingley and his party—"Why, my dear, you must know, Mrs. Long says..."—gaining such momentum in the process that she eventually bubbles out the real point of her enthusiasm:

> A single man of large fortune; four or five thousand a year. What a fine thing for our girls.

Rationals most often regard such Guardian social considerations as unimportant ("trivial" is the Rational's more likely term), and Mr. Bennet finds his wife's excitement over these matters nearly insufferable. Even worse, Rationals grow quickly impatient with spurious reasoning, and Mr. Bennet finds his wife's conclusion completely unsupported and self-serving—she is assuming Bingley's affection and his fortune for her daughter on no objective evidence whatsoever. And so, to express his disapproval of both the subject and the illogical form of her thinking, Mr. Bennet again refuses to let his wife get by with her hidden agenda, forcing her instead to explain herself clearly:

> "How so? how can it [Bingley's arrival] affect them?"
> "My dear Mr. Bennet," replied his wife, "how can you be so tiresome! You must know that I am thinking of his marrying one of them."

As a Provider Guardian, Mrs. Bennet would much rather maneuver her husband through an amiable give-and-take of leading statements and tactful messages—again, what Keirsey calls "implicit roledirectives"[35]—than by coming right out and asserting her plans for young Bingley. But Mr. Bennet's willful refusal to play along effectively unmasks his wife's intention, and then, knowing he has her slightly off-balance, he calls her reasoning further into question, asking sarcastically,

> Is that his design in settling here?[36]

Provider Guardians, however, rarely let their spouse's logic—nor their sarcasm—interfere with their own emotional commitments, and Mrs. Bennet quickly rallies. "Design! nonsense, how can you talk so," she scoffs, dismissing her husband's insensitivity, although she is forced at last to voice the directive implicit in the entire conversation:

> it is very likely that he may fall in love with one of them, and therefore you must visit him as soon as he comes.

Trying to coerce a Definer into acting obediently can be a discouraging experience for a Provider, or indeed for most other types. Rationals as a temperament can be swayed in debate only by a superior argument, and once a Definer is convinced of the logic of his position, he is almost impossible to move. And so in this case, Mr. Bennet simply

---

[35] David Keirsey, *Portraits of Temperament*, p. 14.
[36] Definer Rationals are acutely aware of the *design* or structure of things, particularly of human thought and behavior. See David Keirsey, *Portraits of Temperament*, p. 86.

brushes aside his wife's directive and counters with a more pragmatic solution, pronouncing in his kingly manner,

> You and the girls may go.

Mr. Bennet knows quite well that *he* must initiate such social contacts, and his obstinate flaunting of convention reduces his wife to her Provider's well-known last-device, the accusing appeal for sympathy. "Mr. Bennet," she reproves him, her voice trembling,

> You take delight in vexing me. You have no compassion on my poor nerves.

Rationals are not at all responsive to interpersonal guilt, however, and Mr. Bennet has also borne with his wife's emotional ripostes for far too long to be taken in this easily (even his estate, after all, is known as "Long-bourn"). And so he cleverly turns her complaint back on her, as if taking some droll pleasure in the repartee:

> You mistake me, my dear. I have a high respect for your nerves. They are my old friends. I have heard you mention them with consideration these twenty years at least.

Mrs. Bennet realizes she has lost any hope of making her husband do what she wants and attend to Mr. Bingley, but she cannot resist one parting feint:

> Ah! you do not know what I suffer.[37]

---

[37] This second appeal for sympathy makes it quite clear that Mrs. Bennet's nervous suffering is part of an on-going interpersonal game

On his side, Mr. Bennet knows he has the victory, and can afford to soften his irony with a hint of husbandly conciliation:

> But I hope you will get over it, and live to see many young men of four thousand come into the neighbourhood.

The dubious pleasures of such a crossed-swords relationship was not what either had in mind when they first married. Mrs. Bennet was a fresh, lively young woman, quite popular with the smart young Artisan army officers stationed in her family's neighborhood. "I remember the time," she reminds her husband coyly, "when I liked a redcoat very well"—and then confesses (more wistfully), "so I do still at my heart." But the young Mr. Bennet was so clever and witty, and he had property and a reliable income—just the husband for a young female Provider looking for a proper establishment. On his side, Mr. Bennet married Mrs. Bennet, it seems, very much for her social sparkle. This precise and distant young Rational "was captivated by youth and beauty," Jane Austen reveals, "and that appearance of good humour which youth and beauty generally give." The illusion of love soon ended, however, as Mr. Bennet came to understand the essentially social, *external* cast of his young wife's mind. But instead of appreciating his wife's energy and sociability as valuable differences in style, he defined her as strident and

---

with her family, a game Eric Berne calls "Ain't It Awful." In *Games People Play* (Ballantine ed., 1964), Berne defines the game tactics: "Ain't It Awful" becomes a game...when the player overtly expresses distress, but is covertly gratified at the prospect of the satisfactions he can wring from his misfortune" (p. 112).

superficial, and he began to withold his deepest affections. And now, after some twenty years of contentious marriage, Mrs. Bennet lives largely through her Pygmalion schemes for her husband and daughters, and Mr. Bennet—acting what Jane Austen calls the "true philosopher"—takes his enjoyment in life primarily from his library and from the logical exercise of foiling his wife in family debate.

And so in this case, Mr. Bennet rather cruelly frustrates his wife's most fundamental desire ("the business of her life," as Austen puts it, "was to get her daughters married"), throwing her for several days into a scowling depression. Although Keirsey points out that Providers often take responsibility for their family's problems on their own shoulders,[38] in this case Mrs. Bennet rightfully blames her husband for what she considers her daughter's now-unavoidable spinsterhood. She cannot bear to think of her loss—"I am sick of Mr. Bingley," she cries in her disappointment—though her irritation spills over as well to her neighbors and to her own children. Indeed, she is convinced that her friend Mrs. Long will never be generous enough to introduce Bingley to them of her own accord. "She is a selfish, hypocritical woman," Mrs. Bennet seethes—and most unbearably of all, "she has two nieces of her own." And the slightest provocation from her girls makes Mrs. Bennet bristle with indignation. One evening, "unable to contain herself," Mrs. Bennet suddenly "began scolding one of her daughters":

---

[38] David Keirsey and Marilyn Bates, *Please Understand Me*, p. 193.

Don't keep coughing so, Kitty, for heaven's sake. Have a little compassion for my nerves. You tear them to pieces.[39]

The Provider's anxiety, especially over some galling social failure, can so get the better of them that they will lash out at the least impropriety, trying to regain some sense of control in their lives by asserting their authority, or by pleading their own infirmity. Mr. Bennet steps in at this point, hoping to break the tension in the room by exaggerating the absurdity of his wife's complaint. "Kitty has no discretion in her coughs," he comments dryly; "she times them ill." But Mr. Bennet's wit only antagonizes his wife further, and he knows that to clear the gloom and the acrimony from the air he must confess that he has in fact called on Mr. Bingley, and that a return visit from the young man is quite inevitable.

Mr. Bennet had always intended to welcome his new neighbor—he is curious about Mr. Bingley as a new specimen in the neighborhood—but, of course, he had held back as long as Mrs. Bennet was trying to *make* him to do his social duty. Autonomy is a Rational's point of pride, and now, a fortnight later, feeling rightfully in command of his own actions, he decides to tell Mrs. Bennet of his morning's interview with the young man, and the announcement immediately lifts his wife to new heights of both gratitude and self-congratulations:

---

[39] Jane Austen, *Pride and Prejudice*, p. 4.

> How good it was in you, my dear Mr. Bennet! But I knew I
> should persuade you at last.... Well, how pleased I am![40]

Rationals are uncomfortable with emotional displays, particularly self-flattering ones, and Mr. Bennet strides from the room in the midst of this celebration, "fatigued with the raptures of his wife." Mrs. Bennet, however, realized long ago that if *she* does not sing her own praises, no one will, and so she continues almost without a pause, expounding to the girls the virtues of their father, as well as the unwavering self-sacrifice of their mother:

> What an excellent father you have, girls....I do not know how
> you will ever make him amends for his kindness; or me either,
> for that matter. At our time of life it is not so pleasant, I can
> tell you, to be making new acquaintance everyday; but for
> your sakes, we would do anything.[41]

Keirsey describes how quickly the Provider Guardian's moods of anxiety and depression can brighten, almost of themselves,[42] and hardly before her husband has settled himself again in his library, Mrs. Bennet is organizing a dinner party for the now-incomparable Mr. Bingley, even down to planning "the courses that were to do credit to her housekeeping."

Jane and Mr. Bingley soon meet and, despite her mother's sometimes over-zealous manipulation, begin to fall in love—when by happy chance a second young bachelor

---

[40] Jane Austen, *Pride and Prejudice*, p. 5.

[41] Jane Austen, *Pride and Prejudice*, p. 5.

[42] David Keirsey, *Portraits of Temperament*, p. 62.

enters the neighborhood and promises to solve Mrs. Bennet's other, more long-term problem. Again, since the good woman has had the misfortune (as seen in the eighteenth century) to give birth to five *daughters*, the family will has entailed the Bennet property to a distant male cousin, the Reverend Mr. Collins. Mr. Collins is a gravely formal and scrupulous young Inspector Guardian (an "ISTJ"), and he writes the Bennets quite unexpectedly, asking in the most grandiloquent and obsequious terms to visit them and make amends in advance for the inconvenience he must one day cause them. At first, Mrs. Bennet is flustered and defensive. She refuses even to recognize this "odious man," and on the subject of the iniquitous family will she "was beyond the reach of reason." She soon rallies, however, and chastises her husband, accusing him quite properly of shirking his responsibilities to his own family. "I am sure if I had been you," she fumes, "I should have tried long ago to do something or other about it." But when she calms down and listens to Mr. Collins's letter, with its highly flattering sentiments and its veiled suggestion of an interest in the Bennet girls, she surprises everyone by consenting rather graciously to welcome the young man.

Mr. Collins arrives punctually, and takes up in person where his letter left off. He compliments his hostess in grand fashion; he gives the most unctuous attention to each of her daughters; and he apologizes all over himself for having so impertinently inherited Longbourn. "Mr. Collins" is quite a broad parody of an Inspector Guardian, expressing much of Jane Austen's own Rational amusement with the type, and Mr. Bennet (in his own Rational style) finds his cousin delightfully ridiculous—"as absurd as he had hoped"—and he enjoys himself thoroughly by drawing Collins out on his elegant affectations. Guardians, on the other hand, thoroughly enjoy being admired and appreciated, and a beaming Mrs. Bennet "quarrelled with no compliments" from this gallant young man—though indeed, when he begins to eye the house and the furniture, praising their exquisite qualities, her Provider's possessive nature grows a bit uneasy. "His commendation of everything would have touched Mrs. Bennet's heart," Austen discloses, "but for the mortifying supposition of his viewing it as his own future property."

Mr. Collins wastes no time arranging a private *tête-à-tête* with Mrs. Bennet and presenting his well-considered plan of atonement. He confesses that her daughters are every bit as enchanting in person as they had been "represented by common report" (Inspector Guardians do their research), and that he has his heart set on marrying one of them— Jane, presumably, since she is the oldest and thus satisfies "all his strictest notions of what was due to seniority." Mrs. Bennet's eyes sparkle at this eminently sensible proposal, but she controls herself and, in her most cautious, non-directive style, attempts to steer the love-struck young Inspector away from Jane:

her *eldest* daughter, she must mention—she felt it incumbent on her to hint—was likely to be very soon engaged.

But perhaps, just perhaps, all is not lost. "As to her *younger* daughters," she encourages him with the gentlest smile,

she could not take it upon her to say—she could not positively answer—but she did not *know* of any prepossession.[43]

Mr. Collins quickly adjusts his preferences and agrees that Elizabeth, the second born, would be perfectly agreeable, and Mrs. Bennet quietly thrills to the idea of having two daughters provided for, not to mention the possibility of re-attaching the Bennet property to her side of the family through marriage. In any event, "Mrs. Bennet treasured up the hint" of such success, Austen tells us, "and the man whom she could not bear to speak of the day before was now high in her good graces."

Keirsey observes that Guardians are particularly alert to differences in quantity and degree, noticing relative amounts of things, even in their personal relationships, more acutely than any other temperament.[44] And thus as Mrs. Bennet congratulates herself on her two-fold happiness, she falls quite naturally into a comparison of the value of her two daughters' matrimonial prospects. Jane is all but engaged to the wonderful Mr. Bingley, and

---

[43] Jane Austen, *Pride and Prejudice*, p. 53.
[44] David Keirsey, *Portraits of Temperament*, p. 59.

of having another daughter married to Mr. Collins, she thought with equal certainty, and with considerable, though not equal, pleasure. Elizabeth was the least dear to her of all her children; and though the man and the match were quite good enough for *her*, the worth of each was eclipsed by Mr. Bingley and Netherfield.[45]

Sadly, Mrs. Bennet's most cherished plans for a brilliantly settled future all come crashing down about her ears. (For Guardians, remember, anything that can go wrong, will.) Mr. Bingley suddenly leaves Netherfield to winter in London; and then, in one of fiction's greatest comic scenes, Elizabeth flatly refuses Mr. Collins's ponderous offer of marriage, a proposal filled with solemn assurances of the violence of his affections, as well as with shrewd reminders of his generosity in accepting a young woman whose money earns only "in the 4 per cents." Mrs. Bennet can do nothing about Mr. Bingley's rude departure, but, stunned by this second blow, she vows to fight for Mr. Collins, insisting tearfully that Elizabeth "does not know her own interest; but I will *make* her know it." And so, all in an uproar, Mrs. Bennet hurries instantly to the library, dispensing this time with her role-informative style, and commanding her husband to do his parental duty. "Oh! Mr. Bennet, you are wanted immediately," she cries; "You must come and make Lizzy marry Mr. Collins."

As I have suggested, Rationals deeply resent interpersonal coercion, and for months Mr. Bennet had stayed well clear

---

[45] Jane Austen, *Pride and Prejudice*, p. 78.

of his wife's social maneuverings. Now, however, his territory has been invaded and he must dispatch the enemy as quickly as possible. Mr. Bennet "raised his eyes from his book as she entered, and fixed them on her face with a calm unconcern." He listens quietly to Mrs. Bennet's tirade (she vows never to speak again to her foolish, ungrateful daughter), and he sternly summons Elizabeth to hear his pronouncement on her disobedient conduct, which he delivers with all the precision and symmetry of the Definer Rational at his most articulate:

> An unhappy alternative is before you, Elizabeth. From this day you must be a stranger to one of your parents.—Your mother will never see you again if you do *not* marry Mr. Collins, and I will never see you again if you *do*.[46]

Mrs. Bennet's hopes for any civil cooperation from her husband are thus dashed once again, and feeling thwarted and deceived at every turn, she has little recourse but to deplore her foul mistreatment at the world's hands:

> nobody is on my side, nobody takes part with me, I am cruelly used, nobody feels for my poor nerves.[47]

And later, when she confronts Lizzy for the first time after her unforgivable treatment of Mr. Collins, she promises with great agitation, and at great length, to fulfill her threat of eternal silence:

---

[46] Jane Austen, *Pride and Prejudice*, p. 85.
[47] Jane Austen, *Pride and Prejudice*, p. 85.

you will find me as good as my word. I have no pleasure in talking to undutiful children. Not that I have much pleasure indeed in talking to anybody. People who suffer as I do from nervous complaints can have no great inclination for talking. Nobody can tell what I suffer!—But it is always so. Those who do not complain are never pitied.[48]

Her daughters have learned to listen patiently to such interminable scoldings, knowing "that any attempt to reason with or soothe her would only increase the irritation," and Mrs. Bennet "talked on, therefore, without interruption."

Finally, and even more unhappily, the "steadfast" Mr. Collins quietly abandons Mrs. Bennet, secretly turning his attentions away from the headstrong Elizabeth, and toward his third choice, Charlotte Lucas, the rather homely but more encouraging daughter of Mrs. Bennet's best friend and chief social rival. Mr. Collins sneaks out of Longbourn early one morning and quickly secures Miss Lucas's hand, and Mrs. Bennet is inconsolable when she hears of their treacherous engagement. The "very mention of anything concerning the match threw her into an agony of ill humour," Jane Austen tells us, and Mrs. Bennet announces once and for all, and in "doleful voice," that she "had been barbarously used by them all."

---

[48] Jane Austen, *Pride and Prejudice*, p. 86. Mrs. Bennet's argument for sympathy here frames quite clearly another of Franz Alexander's "emotional syllogisms" of the melancholic depressive (Conservator Artisan) personality: "because I am suffering so much, therefore I deserve to be loved by you." Again, see Alexander's "The Logic of Emotions and Its Dynamic Background," *International Journal of Psychoanalysis*, 16:1935, p. 402.

Pride and Prejudice, as the form of its title suggests, is a beautifully counterbalanced novel, the events of its storyline and the prides and prejudices of its characters skillfully played off against each other. And indeed Mrs. Bennet's carefully nurtured Pygmalion project could not be more thoroughly frustrated. For all her efforts as a Provider, her two daughters are *not* to be married, Longbourn is as much entailed as ever, and—the most galling irony of all—the often slighted Charlotte Lucas will not only be married first, but will eventually inherit all of Mrs. Bennet's jealously guarded possessions. In truth, Mrs. Bennet *has* been barbarously used by them all—by Mr. Bingley, Mr. Collins, Lizzy, Charlotte, and especially by her own husband.

Luckily, Guardians are a resilient temperament, well-practiced in pressing on dutifully through the exasperating twists of fate. And thus, though the novel leaves Mrs. Bennet at this point to nurse her grievances, with Jane Austen's focus shifting to Elizabeth's famous struggles with Rational love (see *The Pygmalion Project, Volume Four*), Mrs. Bennet continues her Pygmalion project behind the scenes, stubbornly battling her daughters' independence and her husband's indifference, asserting again and again in the novel her "earnest desire" to provide, even against their wishes, for her family's moral and material improvement.

*   *   *   *   *

If Babbitt and Mrs. Bennet finally fail to shape their loved ones into responsible Provider Guardians like themselves, it is not for lack of trying, nor does their disappointment go without protest. Protectors might sculpt and suffer in silence, but Providers are more vigorous in their Pygmalion projects, and are not at all shy about voicing their aggravation with an unresponsive mate or child—or as Mrs. Bennet puts it, "Those who do not complain are never pitied." Still, for all their fret and bother—and their occasional guilt-games—Providers are wonderful homemakers, conscientious, vibrant, supportive, and tireless in their efforts to provide for their family's everyday needs. Indeed, Providers fill their lives with *doing* for their family or their community, finding their joy in the routines of social contribution, and often receiving little or no gratitude for their service. And thus, in loving a Provider, we must not belittle the somewhat repetitious *activity* of their providing (as I'm afraid Sinclair Lewis and Jane Austen both do to a certain extent), nor try to stifle their instinct to improve their loved ones and the institutions around them. We must value them for their gifts in sustaining the family and the community, even as we forgive them their predisposition to impress their own sensibilities—their Guardian *shoulds* and *shouldn'ts*—on our lives.

Chapter 4

The Inspector

> It came over him that it was because she took things hard she had sought his acquaintance; it had been because she was strenuous, not because she was genial; she had had in her eye—and what an extraordinary eye it was!—not a pleasure but a duty. She would expect him to be strenuous in return...
>
> ———Henry James[1]

The Monitor Guardians are similar in many ways to their cousins the Conservator Guardians. Both temperaments are earnest in their conduct of life, both are traditional in their attitudes, both dutiful and dependable in their actions, and they are even similarly group or family-centered in their social relations. However, the two differ significantly in their styles of interaction. If Conservators care for their loved ones somewhat tenderly or indulgently, Monitors are more adament in their guardianship, more impatient with

---

[1] Henry James, *The Bostonians* (Modern Library ed., 1956), p. 18.

their loved ones' character flaws and misdeeds. Furthermore, if Conservators prefer *complying* with their loved
ones' demands, hoping to manage their relationships with
as little conflict as possible, Monitors are more *commanding* with their loved ones, more than willing to tell
them what to do and when to do it. Monitors are thus what
Keirsey calls the role-directive[2] Guardians, and the names
he has given them—Inspectors (Myers's "ISTJ's") and
Supervisors ("ESTJ's")—clearly indicate their more stren-
uous commitment to interpersonal coercion. Of course, the
less gregarious Inspectors are less aggressive in their
Pygmalion projects than the Supervisors, certainly less vol-
uble, though no less tenacious. Keirsey observes that
Inspectors are typically the sober, plain-speaking, "pillar of
strength" in their relationships,[3] but the evidence of literature suggests that while their support for their partners is
unusually steadfast, so quite often is their determination to
"re-form" them in their own image.

Rose Sayer

Literature rarely presents the Inspector Guardian in a
sympathetic light, particularly if the Inspector is a woman.
By far the more common characterization of the female
Inspector emphasizes her dark side: she is the nagging,
carping shrew-wife, introduced in many stories merely to
establish dramatic conflict and to motivate her husband's

---

[2] David Keirsey, *Portraits of Temperament*, p. 44.
[3] David Keirsey and Marilyn Bates, *Please Understand Me*, pp. 190-191.

longing for freedom. Flaubert's ruthless little sketch of Madame Dubuc, Charles Bovary's first wife in *Madame Bovary*, is sadly typical:

> Charles had envisaged marriage as the beginning of a better time, thinking that he would have greater freedom and be able to do as he liked with himself and his money. But it was his wife who ruled: in front of company he had to say certain things and not others, he had to eat fish on Friday, dress the way she wanted, obey her when she ordered him to dun nonpaying patients. She opened his mail, watched his every move, and listened through the thinness of the wall when there were women in the office.
>
> She had to have her cup of chocolate every morning: there was no end to the attentions she required. She complained incessantly of her nerves, of pains in her chest, of depressions and faintnesses....When Charles came home in the evening she would bring her long thin arms out from under her bedclothes, twine them around his neck, draw him down beside her on the edge of the bed, and launch into the tale of her woes.[4]

Such meanspirited caricatures might be technically useful to the (generally male) novelist or playwright, but they are hardly fair to real-life female Inspectors, who usually get after their men only with the best of intentions, trying to keep them from frittering their lives away and to help them live more responsibly and considerately. C.S. Forester, oddly enough, since he was well-known as a writer of men's adventure stories, was one novelist who saw past the negative stereotype, and managed to portray one of the most attractive female Inspectors in all of fiction: Rose Sayer in *The African Queen*.

---

[4] Gustave Flaubert, *Madame Bovary*, trans. Francis Steegmuller (The Modern Library ed., 1957), p. 13.

Rose Sayer is a thirty-three year old Englishwoman, straight-laced and strong-minded, who has spent the last ten years of her "frozen spinsterhood" keeping house for her brother Samuel, a Christian missionary in German Central Africa. When the Kaiser's army loots the mission and conscripts all the nearby villagers in its arrogant preparation for World War I, Samuel prays for heavenly guidance and then dies of fever and of grief, and Rose is left to fend for herself, "alone in the Central African forest, alone with a dead man." Though expert at managing her brother's household, Rose is not used to directing her own life; she "came from a stratum of society and of history," Forester reminds us, "in which woman adhered to her menfolk's opinions," and at first she is overwhelmed by the loss of masculine structure in her life. But in the dim hours after Samuel's death, faced with her own grave peril, Rose throws off her demoralization and her fear, and settles firmly on her duty. Guardians, with their belief in traditional authority, can be fervently patriotic, devoted to King and country, and Rose (dressed as always in her "white drill frock") decides she must somehow "strike a blow for England" against the forces of "the Hun." She is not quite certain how to do this, and even frowns "with scorn of herself for daydreaming," but her resolve hardens with the set of her jaw. Her brother was dead and "the Empire was in danger," and she clenches her mouth "like a trap into its usual hard line."

Rose's determination to strike back at Germany finds a reluctant ally in Charlie Allnut, a Cockney mining mechanic fleeing the Germans himself in a dilapidated river launch named, ironically, the *African Queen*. Charlie is a stubbly, grimy little man, smelling of gear oil and gin, with a battered sun hat and a cigarette hanging from his upper lip—a species of man that Samuel had "set his face sternly against as an unchristian example." Charlie is also a crafty, resourceful Instrumentalist Artisan (an "ISTP"), who has made off with the clumsy old steam launch, along with a whole boatload of food and gin and mining supplies, to wait out the war in the marshy backwater of the Ulanga River. As an Instrumentalist, Charlie is a virtuoso with all kinds of mechanical devices—for him, Forester observes, "there was even an aesthetic pleasure" in patching and prodding the *African Queen's* leaky old boiler into service. Indeed, Charlie "was a man of machinery, a man of facts, not of fancies," and when he stops at the mission for news of the Germans, he "had not the remotest idea of striking a blow for England." Charlie's notion, on the contrary, "had been to put the maximum possible distance between himself and the struggle," and he urges Rose to join him on the *African Queen* out of an impulsive generosity—and a practical need for help with the boat—happily unaware of her patriotic intentions.

As many of you know from John Huston's famous film of *The African Queen*, the novel tells the story of how this Guardian-Artisan odd couple navigate down the perilous Ulanga to attack the *Königen Louise*, a huge German police boat that patrols the strategic Lake Wittelsbach basin. But the novel is also about how this prim, ladylike spinster and this dirty, hard-drinking mechanic-of-all-work negotiate past their initial antagonism and fall in love. Running rapids and avoiding German lookouts and fashioning torpedoes by hand is the grand adventure in the novel, but just as gripping is Forester's remarkable depiction of the repulsions and attractions in the Inspector-Instrumentalist relationship.

Rose and Charlie's immediate point of conflict, very simply, is that both Inspectors and Instrumentalists are role-directive types, and thus they must spar a bit to determine who controls the relationship. Once on board the *African Queen*, for example, Rose tries almost at once to take command of the wiry little Cockney, much as she grasps the tiller of the boat:

> Rose silently took hold of the iron rod….She held it resolutely, with almost a thrill at feeling the *African Queen* waver obediently in her course as she shifted the tiller ever so little.[5]

Rose begins asking Allnut leading questions about his knowledge of the river, and he answers decisively, trying to regain control of the relationship and to re-direct the conversation (not to mention the boat) into safer channels:

> "Allnutt," she said. "This river, the Ulanga, runs into the lake, doesn't it?"
> The question was a disquieting one.

---

[5] C.S. Forester, *The African Queen* (Boston, 1968), p. 20. All quotations are from this edition.

"Well, Miss, it does. But if you was thinking of going to the lake in this launch—well, you needn't think about it any more. We can't, and that's certain."[6]

Unimpressed, Rose scans the *African Queen* for combat materiel and interrogates Allnut about his knowledge of explosives, while he ("conscious of her scrutiny") tries to dampen her enthusiasm before she gets up a dangerous head of steam:

"What are those boxes with the red lines on them?" she demanded.
"That's the blasting gelatine I told you about, Miss."
"Isn't it dangerous?"
"Coo, bless you, Miss, no." Allnutt was glad of the opportunity to display his indifference in the presence of this woman who was growing peremptory and uppish. "This is safety stuff, this is.... I'll put it over the side if it worries you, though."
"No!" said Rose, sharply. "We may want it."[7]

Rose's mind is racing all through this interchange, formulating some vague plan of retribution against the Germans, but Forester is careful to point out that such rebellious and inventive thinking "was not easy" for her. As an essentially orthodox Inspector Guardian, Rose has a "methodical mind," needing "to complete one step before thinking about the next," and thus as she tries to concentrate on how to punish the Germans, "two vertical lines showed between her thick eyebrows." However, Rose makes up in

---

[6] C.S. Forester, *The African Queen*, p. 29.
[7] C.S. Forester, *The African Queen*, p. 35.

determination what she lacks in strategical ingenuity; she finally sees her way and triumphantly announces her plan: "'All right,' said Rose. 'We'll go down to the lake and torpedo the *Louisa*.'"

In a contest of role-directive messages, an obstinate, upright Inspector will usually overpower a more impulsive Instrumentalist, and indeed Charlie decides he had better switch tactics with Rose. "It might be as well to temporize," he thinks, "just to humour her." And so, for the time being, Charlie gives in to Rose's direction, and Forester ingeniously reveals his motives. First of all, with his Artisan bravado, Charlie is not willing to admit publically that he is a coward and "would not lift a hand for England." At the same time, with his Artisan aimlessness, Charlie is quite willing to let Rose take charge of the journey, if it will make her happy:

> Sooner than plan or work for himself he preferred to be guided—or driven. He was not avid for responsibility. He was glad to hand over leadership to those who desired it, even to the ugly sister of a deceased, despised missionary.[8]

Charlie also has the Artisan gambler's optimism that, if he is patient, "something else [will] turn up" to spoil Rose's mission and return control to him. Of course, he has some aces up his sleeve. He knows that the dangers and snags on the river will likely frighten Rose off her scheme, or "failing that, he hoped for an unspectacular and safe

---

[8] C.S. Forester, *The African Queen*, pp. 41-42.

shipwreck which would solve the problem for them." And he knows how unreliable the *African Queen's* engines are—or ("happy thought") how easily he could sabotage them. However, at bottom, Charlie submits to Rose because of his Artisan capacity for living in the present moment. Rose's plan is surely unworkable—even suicidal—but,

> anyway, there were two hundred miles of comfortable river ahead before the rapids began, and Allnutt's temperament was such that anything a week off was hardly worth worrying about.[9]

Charlie thus acquiesces—"'Ave it yer own wye, then, Miss"—though, to do him justice, not without a last role-directive warning: "Only don't blame me. That's all."

The first day on the river Rose and Charlie stay rather politely out of each other's way. He tends the engine with an amazing Instrumentalist agility, and she, an Inspector with "a firmer grip on the tiller," peers forward "with narrowed eyelids over the glaring surface of the river," searching the channel for snags and obstructions. However, at dusk, when Charlie anchors the boat out of sight and pulls out his gin bottle, Rose begins to fear for her life—and her virtue. "Drink made men madmen," she staunchly believes; "drink rotted their bodies and corrupted their souls," and she glares at Charlie with all her Guardian disdain for self-indulgence. Ironically, Rose has her own weakness for drink, only in her case it is tea, and she

---

[9] C.S. Forester, *The African Queen*, p. 43.

observes her ritual with an almost religious devotion. "Twelve cups of tea...she had drunk daily for years," Forester tells us, and when Charlie offers her a cup, brewed with boiler water and sweetened with condensed milk, the prospect "roused her to trembling excitement," and she "drank it strong, mug after mug of it." In any event, Charlie keeps his distance, even under the influence of demon gin, and promises to sleep up front, on top of the explosives, while Rose (warmed by the tea) relaxes her vigilance somewhat and prepares her Guardian bed on the *African Queen's* hard and narrow stern deck.

The next few days of working together on the *African Queen*, verging at times on unexpectedly pleasant companionship, end abruptly as Rose and Charlie approach the German lookout point at Shona, after which the river falls away into miles of boiling, impassable rapids. Charlie seems restless and sulky on their last night's safe anchor, and is drinking one cup of gin after another—until Rose "looked sharply at him," and he confesses the truth of the matter. He has decided to end her fool's scheme, and he tells her shakily, "We ain't goin' no further down the river." Rose listens, "white with angry disappointment," and she pleads with Charlie to have more faith in their mission, finally calling him a coward to his face. But he will not be bullied this time, and he proceeds to get roaring drunk, tossing down several more gins "to set the seal on his resolution." Rose has never had to confront such sullen inertia before, and gathering herself bitterly in the sternsheets, she broods over her course of action: "She resolved, as the night wore on, to make Allnutt pay for his arbitrariness. She set her teeth...as she swore to herself to make Allnut's life hell for him."

Rose's ensuing Pygmalion project to sober Charlie up and make him do his duty for England is as close as Forester comes in the novel to casting her in literature's malicious stereotype. Indeed, as she sits all night clenched in her "cold rage," Forester describes Rose as "a shrew, a woman with the temper of a fiend," and he reveals her austere pride in her "ability to nag," convinced that "nagging was the only...practicable method of making Allnutt's life hell for him." Still, for all her righteous anger with Charlie, by morning Rose has settled on a more civilized, and vastly more interesting, tactic for making him see things her way, an elegant torture Forester calls "the great silence."

Thus, when Charlie regains consciousness the next morning, he finds Rose systematically emptying his store of gin bottles over the side. He protests as forcibly as he is able, but Rose "paid no attention to his moaning and whimpering," and proceeds to pour out bottle after bottle, dropping the empties into the brown river. That done, she tidies herself up "without paying him the least attention," and then prepares her breakfast giving "him neither look nor word," and then eats alone "with perfect composure."

Charlie ("sick and white and trembling") hasn't the strength to be bothered much at first, but as the day grows hotter and

his mind clears, he attempts to make friendly conversation—"Coo, ain't it 'ot?"—while Rose sits quietly at her
sewing, simulating "complete absorption" in her buttons
and threads. Feeling chastised and a bit bewildered, Charlie
tries several times to make conversation, but only once is
Rose moved to respond. "I hate you," she spits at him;
"You're a coward and you tell lies and [sounding much like
Mrs. Bennet in *Pride and Prejudice*] I won't speak to you
ever." Charlie assumes that Rose is angry about his
drinking, and after several more unsuccessful offers to
make up, he tries to break the silence by apologizing:

> "Ain't yer goin' to answer me, Miss?" he said—and then, still
> eliciting no notice, he went on—"I'm sorry for what I done
> last night. There! I don't mind sayin' it."[10]

Instead of restoring their companionship, however,
Charlie's more or less sincere repentance only gives Rose
some idea of the interpersonal power at her disposal, and
steels her determination to resurrect her sacred mission.
Rose had originally hoped only to punish Charlie for his
cowardice and inconstancy, but when he "began to ask for
mercy," Forester tells us, "it dawned upon her that she
might be able to coerce him into obeying her."

The paradox of being pointedly ignored[11] infuriates almost
all the types, but Rose's silent treatment is particularly

---

[10] C.S. Forester, *The African Queen*, p. 92.

[11] The tactic's baffling frustration lies in its self-contradiction: the
message is in not receiving a message, the scolding is in not being
scolded. The recipient (or victim) is caught in a classic "double
bind" situation: he cannot tell what the message is, so he cannot

effective with an Instrumentalist Artisan. Instrumentalists are innately social creatures, quite lost without human interaction or social impact. Keirsey puts it even more forcefully: for all the Artisans, "to be totally without influence, to make no difference at all in human affairs, is like being deprived of oxygen."[12] Of course, Charlie, tactically stalling for time, had let Rose take control at the beginning of the journey; but when he finally asserts himself, and is met with Rose's blank disregard, he loses his temper at his own impotence in the face of this intractable woman: "'Ave it yer own wye, then, yer psalm-singing ole bitch."

Charlie calms down a bit and decides that two can play at this game, and so he attempts to go about his business and see how *Rose* likes being ignored. First he busies himself with overhauling the engine, and then he makes a big show of washing himself thoroughly, and even of shaving his stubble. Once again, however, Charlie is at a distinct disadvantage in what Forester calls this "duel" of silence with Rose. Forester observes that as an Instrumentalist Charlie "had always had companions in his leisure periods," and that "solitude was as distressing to him as responsibility." And he is soon at his wits' end trying to amuse himself, "cooped, compulsorily, in a thirty foot

---

respond appropriately—hence the rage. See Gregory Bateson's article, "Toward a Theory of Schizophrenia" in *Steps To an Ecology of Mind* (New York, 1972), pp. 201-227.

[12] David Keirsey, *Portraits of Temperament*, p. 19.

boat," with nothing to do except listen to the gurgle of the river. Rose, with her Inspector's discipline and linear mentality, is perfectly comfortable with such change-lessness, content to sit in silence counting her grievances. But the monotony is maddening to an Instrumentalist— "Silence was one of the things he could not endure"—and Forester calls the Artisan's need for variety and social impact a "natural disability" in such a contest. Charlie, Forester understands,

> had never been accustomed to doing any continuous thinking, so that in a situation in which there was nothing to do but think he was helpless.[13]

Charlie soon begins to crack under the strain of silence and inaction: "He shifted and twisted and turned... he sat up and smoked cigarettes; he fidgeted." And slowly he comes to fathom the real objective of Rose's Pygmalion project: although it means their certain death, she wants to continue her mission. "Rose was earnest about it," Charlie realizes with amazement (and a certain admiration), "and... would give him no word and no look until he agreed to it." And so, finally, troubled with insomnia and a "slightly disordered digestion," Charlie knows he must give in: "Let's 'ear wotcha wanter do, Miss. Tell us, and we'll do it. There, Miss."

Rose and Charlie's mad dash through the German machine gun fire at Shona, which then sweeps them headlong into the rocks and whirlpools of the lower rapids on the Ulanga,

---

[13] C.S. Forester, *The African Queen*, p. 95.

is the most exhilarating episode in *The African Queen*—it is Forester at his best in the novel. But their shared danger and their back-breaking victory over the rapids bring Rose and Charlie more than mere excitement. They each discover a courage under fire and pride in their achievement that bonds them like comrades-in-arms. And as they lie exhausted on the deck, savoring their impossible survival, they also find—and quite wondrously—that they love each other.

Forester does not dwell in much detail, nor very perceptively, on Rose and Charlie's physical passion—he is not D.H. Lawrence—but his analysis of the curious basis of the Guardian-Artisan attraction is profound. On one level, Rose's heart-stopping adventure with Charlie has emancipated her body and inflamed a long-repressed sexual desire. Her harrowing brush with Artisan danger on board the *African Queen* "was a sensation intoxicating in its novelty," Forester tells us, and adds that her once-frigid body now "seethed with life." As I have argued several times (in this book and in *Volume One*), the inherently cautious Guardian is quite often drawn to the freedom and invigoration of an Artisan mate, and indeed, caught up in the joyous celebration of their miraculous accomplishment, Rose soon finds herself in Charlie's arms, eagerly pressing his "slight body" to her own.

But more deeply, and with wonderful insight, Forester explains that Rose falls in love with Charlie not only out of a new-found sexual desire, but out of her Guardian parental

instinct as well. Rose shares the nineteenth century Englishwoman's largely Guardian belief that men were a helpless,
childish sex, and that women's time-honored role was faithfully "to devote themselves to clearing their path for them
and smoothing their way":

> Their trivial illnesses must be coddled, their peevish
> complaints heard with patience, their bad temper condoned.[14]

In other words, Rose sees Charlie not only as a man to be
loved but as a child to be cared for, and her attraction to
him is as much maternal as it is sensual. At first, as they
rest next to each other in the bow, recovering from the
rapids, Rose looks at Charlie and confesses that "There was
something appealing, almost childlike, about the little man
with his dazed smile. She wanted to pet him." And later,
after they have embraced and "done their will" upon each
other, as Forester rather stiffly puts it, Rose begins to see
Charlie's Artisan imperfections—his drunkenness and
carelessness and lack of fortitude—as unavoidable male
shortcomings, quite boyish and actually endearing. And she
senses, finally, that her own deepest satisfaction as a
woman will be in mothering this flawed and forlorn little
Cockney, and not in trying to perfect him through a more
scathing Pygmalion project:

---

[14] C.S. Forester, *The African Queen*, p. 138.

> And these very frailties of his made an insidious appeal to the maternal part of her, and so did his corporal frailty, and the hard luck he had always experienced.[15]

Rose's sudden willingness to coddle Charlie in his weaknesses might strike the modern reader as a sorry come down for her, perhaps even betraying some typically Victorian male-chauvinistic attitude on Forester's part. But remember that all her life Rose has been contentedly keeping house for some man, first for her father, and then for her brother Samuel. And remember as well that, more than any other temperament, female Guardians regard family duty as the deepest expression of their love, often giving it a greater importance than sexual intimacy.[16] And thus Forester is quite right, especially at the time of his story, to emphasize the uniquely *maternal* nature of Rose's love for Charlie, which intensifies even as her sexual passion wanes. "As the flame of passion died down," Forester observes, "she was happy, and cradled him in her strong arms."

For his part, "Allnutt was very happy too." As an Artisan, he takes particular pleasure in initiating Rose sexually, but Forester is careful to point out that, "whatever [Charlie] might do in the heat of passion, his need was just as much

---

[15] C.S. Forester, *The African Queen*, p. 139.

[16] As Keirsey puts it: "For the female SJ [Guardian] especially one who is introverted, home may be a focal point, to the exclusion of all else. Devotion to husband and children, the preparation of meals, keeping a clean and orderly house may take all her time and become her reason for living," *Please Understand Me*, pp. 84-85.

for a mother as a mistress." Indeed, and reciprocally, Artisans often seek out Guardian mates for the parental security of their love (Artisan husbands even have a habit of referring to their Guardian wives as "Mother"), as if aware that they need a stable, reliable center to their lives. Thus, held secure in Rose's arms, Charlie "felt he could trust her and depend upon her as he had never trusted or depended on a woman in his life." And the next morning, when Rose gets up, fixes him breakfast, and then resumes control of the expedition, Charlie "was quite happy to cast all the responsibility onto her shoulders." In this way, Rose and Charlie—female and male, but also mother and child—create one of the most balanced Guardian-Artisan relationships I have found in literature, both partners relenting in their Pygmalion projects, and finding a joyous fulfillment in each other *as they are*.

The remainder of the journey down the Ulanga River to Lake Wittelsbach is more arduous than exhilarating, marked by a mangled propeller shaft, days on end trapped in the stagnant, reed-choked delta, bouts with unbearable heat and malaria, and finally the utter failure of Rose's scheme, as the *African Queen* sinks in the lake before it can even approach the *Königen Luise*, throwing her and Charlie into the hands of the German navy. But all through these ordeals, Rose and Charlie manage to maintain the delicate Inspector-Instrumentalist balance in their relationship. Rose both bosses Charlie around and fusses over him like his mother. "No, you sit down and rest yourself," she orders him in one typical scene, "and mind you don't catch cold."

And Charlie both obeys ("there was no denying Rose") and remains master of his own domain, deftly improvising to keep the *African Queen* moving ahead, even taking a "primitive pleasure," as Forester calls it, in forging a new propeller blade from spare boiler metal. They also take time to explore their passion, and Rose discovers that "the sensation of intimacy with Charlie, combatting piquantly with her modesty, was extraordinarily pleasant." To be sure, Rose is amazed by the complementary nature of their affection, both emotionally and sexually:

> She had never realized before that friendliness and merriment could exist along with a serious purpose in life, any more than she had realized that there was pleasure in the intercourse of the sexes. There was something intensely satisfying in their companionship.[17]

Rose has her Guardian guilts, of course. On their last night in the channel, coming clear finally of the reeds and mud, Rose is awakened from Charlie's side by an agonizing recognition of her own sinfulness:

> She had lain with a man in unlicensed lust. For a moment she remembered with shocked horror the things she had done with that man, her wanton immodesty. It made matters worse that she had actually *enjoyed* it, as no woman should ever dream of doing.[18]

Conscience-stricken, Rose climbs to her knees, clasps her hands, and in a "passion of remorse" prays to God for forgiveness. Rose's quiet weeping slowly rouses Charlie,

---

[17] C.S. Forester, *The African Queen*, p. 163.
[18] C.S. Forester, *The African Queen*, p. 238.

and though he watches her bowed figure in the moonlight, is indeed "awed by the sight" of such sincere repentance, he has little interest in heavenly sanction, and gladly leaves the rituals of atonement to Rose. Artisans rarely lose much sleep with a guilty conscience, and in this case Forester observes that, snug in his easy peace of mind, Charlie's eyes soon close, "and he drifted off again, leaving Rose to bear her agony alone."

For all their fulfillment on board the *African Queen,* then, Rose and Charlie still have deep-seated temperamental differences to overcome in their relationship, as the ending of the novel even more clearly suggests. When the Germans finally turn Rose and Charlie over to the English and Belgian forces, Rose realizes that they have ended their private jungle adventure and must face their future back in Christian civilization. For the present, Charlie promises to enlist in a South African unit against the Germans, and Rose is set to return to England—to explain herself, she knows full well, to "censorious people and prying aunts." Faced with her lost virtue and her unavoidable separation from Charlie, Rose's Guardian conscience weighs heavily on her again, and "seething with shame" she quickly proposes their only honorable course:

> "Charlie," she said urgently. "We've got to get married."
> "Coo," said Allnutt. This was an aspect of the situation he actually had not thought of... [and] this new proposal left him with hardly a word to say.[19]

---

[19] C.S. Forester, *The African Queen*, pp. 307-308.

Charlie, naturally, couldn't care less about observing social or religious forms, but he does have his own practical Artisan interests *and* his past indiscretions to consider:

> He thought of Rose's moderate superiority in social status. He thought about money....He thought about the girl he had married twelve years ago...there had never been a divorce and presumably he was still married to her.

Taking internal inventory in this way is not Charlie's strong suit, nor is he inclined to stand on scruple concerning bigamy, and so he cheerfully decides once again to go along with Rose's plan for him:

> Oh well, South Africa and England were a long way apart, and she couldn't trouble him much.
> "Righto, Rosie," he said, "let's."[20]

Forester has brought Rose and Charlie in *The African Queen* from mutual disgust to ardent companionship, and finally to the brink of marriage, but he knows too much about Inspector bossiness and Instrumentalist impulsiveness to press his luck. And thus in the novel's cautious last sentence, Forester leaves us with this uncertain forecast: "Whether or not they lived happily ever after is not easily decided."

Gertrude Morel

The Inspector Guardians' desire to reform their loved ones is called forth even more graphically in relationships with

---

[20] C.S. Forester, *The African Queen*, p. 308.

their exact opposites among the Artisans, the Performers ("ESFP's"). Inspectors are often drawn to Performers for their Dionysian sense of freedom and spontaneity, the joy of letting go, and they can find remarkable satisfaction in the complementarity of such a match.[21] However, when the Inspector tires of the exuberance and the publicity of the relationship—living on stage, in the spotlight—and undertakes to tame the Performer into a sensible, responsible partner, the collision of temperaments can be dreadful. I examined a tumultuous Inspector-Performer marriage from the Artisan's point-of-view in *Volume One* of *The Pygmalion Project*, describing the hostility and self-destructiveness of Walter Morel in D.H. Lawrence's *Sons and Lovers*. At this time I want to return to Lawrence's magnificent novel to look more carefully at Gertrude Morel's side of the story, and at the more desperate tactics of love and coercion for the female Inspector Guardian.

Gertrude Morel was born Gertrude Coppard, the second daughter of a "good old burgher family," stout Congregationalists who went bankrupt in the collapse of the Nottingham lace-market in the middle of the nineteenth century. Her father, George Coppard (a Supervisor Guardian), grew up to become foreman at the dockyard, but Gertrude remembers that he was "bitterly galled" by his low station in life, and that, at home, he ruled his wife with an iron hand. George Coppard was "harsh in government," a strict theologian in his reading, and one who "ignored all

---

[21] David Keirsey and Marilyn Bates, *Please Understand Me*, p. 78.

sensuous pleasure" in his life, and though Gertrude despised her father's "overbearing manner towards her gentle, humorous, kindly-souled mother," Lawrence leaves little doubt that Gertrude inherited much of his stringent temperament. Lawrence tells us that, no matter how much Gertrude loved her mother and defended her, she nevertheless had her father's "temper, proud and unyielding," and she looked on at the world around her with his "clear, defiant blue eyes."

Gertrude was a bright child and, in typical Guardian style, a conscientious student. She "loved to help" manage her classroom, eventually becoming an assistant to the old schoolmistress, and her solemn, bookish manner earned her the reputation in the Erewash Valley of being "very intellectual." Let me clarify this point about "intellect" among the temperaments. Keirsey argues that each temperament has its own intellectual strengths and weaknesses, or rather its natural hierarchy of mental skills. Artisans are most gifted in composing sensual variations, Rationals in analyzing complex abstract structures, Idealists in interpreting and integrating metaphorical implications, and Guardians in examining and measuring the social world.[22] Like most authors, Lawrence at times combines these four types of intellect in his characters, but in Gertrude's case he emphasizes that she had a particularly "curious, receptive mind" for the social world around her; she prefered to read books on

---

[22] David Keirsey, *Portraits of Temperament*, pp. 23 and 35; 69 and 81; 92 and 104; and 47 and 58, in that order.

"social questions," and was especially "clever in leading folk to talk...about themselves"—examining them in a sense. Let me add that Inspectors are also intellectually contentious, and seem to enjoy heated disputes over burning social issues, not so much to settle the issues as to make sure that they have thoroughly discussed significant topics. And thus as she grew older Gertrude found that what she "liked most of all was an argument on religion or philosophy or politics with some educated man," and later, as an adult, she joined the "Women's Guild," a discussion group devoted to social reform.

In any event, Gertrude grew up a serious, studious, severe young woman, "of delicate mould but resolute bearing," invariably dressed in plain dark blue silk, and "rather contemptuous" of frivolities such as jewelry and dancing— "She was puritan, like her father," Lawrence stresses again, "high-minded and really stern." Indeed, with her education and her exacting temperament, Gertrude held herself socially and intellectually above her neighbors. She assumed "a kind of aristocracy" among the local townsfolk, rarely condescending to associate with the common young farmers and miners in the valley, much preferring to observe the social life around her with her "straight, honest, and searching" gaze.

At twenty-three, Gertrude is "still perfectly intact" in her strict superiority, when she happens to meet Walter Morel, a handsome young coalminer, at the valley Christmas party.

As I described him in *Volume One*, Walter is an archetypal male Performer Artisan, flirting with all the girls at the party, jollying his buddies with his good-natured taunting and mimicry, laughing his "rich, ringing laugh," and dancing every dance "as if it were natural and joyous in him to dance." Gertrude Coppard had never "met anyone like him" Lawrence tells us, and she "thought him rather wonderful," not a precise and satirical man like her father, but vibrant and sensual, with a "subtle exultation like glamour in his movement... laughing alike whatever partner he bowed above." Gertrude sits "fascinated," watching the young miner spread his animal warmth and good humor throughout the room, and Lawrence makes it clear that Gertrude is drawn almost in spite of herself to his fundamental *difference* in temperament. Morel is a Performer Artisan, "soft, non-intellectual, warm," and Lawrence states flatly that Gertrude "herself was opposite," a hard, mindful, rather frigid Inspector Guardian. And yet, despite the enormous distance between them, she suddenly longs to give herself up to Morel's irresistible radiance:

> the dusky, golden softness of this man's sensuous flame of life, that flowed off his flesh like the flame of a candle, not gripped into incandescence by thought and spirit as her life was, seemed to her something wonderful, beyond her.[23]

The attraction is much more physically passionate, of course, than Gertrude is willing to admit, though again and again in this scene Lawrence hints at her growing

---

[23] D.H. Lawrence, *Sons and Lovers* (Penguin ed., 1981), p. 10. All quotations are from this edition.

awareness of Morel's compelling sexuality. At first, the strutting young miner strikes her as "well set-up, erect," then she can't help noticing his black-bearded cheeks and his "red, moist mouth," and eventually she stares quite openly at "his face, the flower of his body, ruddy, with tumbled black hair." Sadly, Inspectors all too often repress their Dionysian responses, and when Morel finally stops and smiles above her, urging her to try a dance with him— "It's easy, you know"—she can only keep her head and refuse him in her stubborn, decisive way: "'No, I won't dance'....Her words came clean and ringing."

For his part, Morel is just as uneasily attracted to Gertrude—*his* opposite—a straight-laced Inspector Guardian. Though he loves to tease and flirt with the local farming and shop girls, Gertrude's prim manner and her proper, educated speech thrill him in a way he has never known, suddenly arresting his playfulness and dissolving his swaggering Artisan confidence:

> Walter Morel seemed melted away before her. She was to the miner that thing of mystery and fascination, a lady.[24]

Artisans, of course, rarely resist their impulses, and even though Gertrude chides him rather irritably that he's missing his dance, Morel finds himself inexplicably pulled to her side:

> Not knowing what he was doing—he often did the right thing by instinct—he sat beside her, inclining reverentially.[25]

---

[24] D.H. Lawrence, *Sons and Lovers*, p. 9.
[25] D.H. Lawrence, *Sons and Lovers*, p. 10.

Many of Lawrence's fictions offer some version of this magnetic confrontation, the Guardian woman and the Artisan man held paradoxically in the grip of each other's dissimilarity. And often Lawrence goes on in his stories to explore the incomprehensible sexual fulfillment that such a mating of opposites can bring the Guardian woman, as she learns to burn away her traditional, tightly ritualized consciousness—to trust her instincts and to relinquish herself to the joyous knowledge of the senses, what Lawrence called the Artisan's "blood consciousness." Indeed, Lawrence's considerable genius as a novelist lies in his almost poetic ability to make the dark, pre-conscious mysteries of the body—the blind touch of flesh and the sinuous energy of our sexual nature—somehow *comprehensible* in language. We read Lawrence's hypnotic prose and we understand how it must feel to live in the rapturous dark, by our physical senses, guided only by the flame of our primal passions.

Inspector Guardians, however, with their more deliberate concern for *scrutinizing* reality, have a particularly difficult time giving themselves up to this sensual flame in the darkness, and when Morel sits next to Gertrude and describes his life in the coalmine—"You live like th' mice, an' you pop out at night to see what's going on"—she instinctively clings to her secure daylight world of social consciousness, answering him with a shudder: "It makes me feel blind." And yet, again, it is just this glimpse of a more primitive, ravishing darkness that thrills Gertrude and makes the young miner so seductive. Lawrence tells us that, after hearing of Morel's brutal yet strangely exhilarating life "toiling below earth," Gertrude humbles herself before such Dionysian sensuality and, "with a touch of appeal in her pure humility," she closes her eyes and begins to fall in love.

Gertrude and Walter marry the following Christmas, and in their first few months together they seem rather happily to meet each other halfway. Gertrude, first of all, gives Morel some occasion for order and discipline. He refurnishes his house with "solid, worthy stuff that suited her honest soul"; he makes quite a show of giving up his drinking and dancing at the pubs; and he also seems content to busy himself around the house, turning his Artisan talents to more domestic purposes: "He was a remarkably handy man—could make or mend anything." On his side, Walter gives his wife perhaps the greatest of Artisan gifts, the joy of passion. Much later in the novel, after years of alienation, Walter can still see the glow of "the passion she had had for him. It blazed upon her for a moment"; and their son Paul can tell that, despite his parents' bitter differences,

> my mother, I believe, got real joy and satisfaction out of my father at first. I believe she had a passion for him... the real flame of feeling through another person—once, only once, if it only lasts three months.[26]

---

[26] D.H. Lawrence, *Sons and Lovers*, p. 317.

However, for an Inspector Guardian a few months of sexual passion, no matter how sublime, is indeed a short-lived and rather frivolous basis for such a serious relationship as marriage. And Lawrence very soon reveals Gertrude's first painful moments of caution and alarm, when she glimpses the truth that, no matter how physically bonded they are, she and Walter will never share much more than their sexuality:

> Sometimes, when she herself wearied of love-talk, she tried to open her heart seriously to him. She saw him listen deferentially, but without understanding. This killed her efforts at a finer intimacy, and she had flashes of fear.[27]

These initial misgivings flare into a terrible resentment quite suddenly one Sunday when Gertrude, brushing Walter's church coat, discovers the unpaid bills for the furniture, and the next day she investigates and finds out that he had lied about owning his house—he pays rent to his mother, and a good deal more than the place is worth. Gertrude is stunned at her husband's seemingly casual duplicity. She had believed Walter to be a man of virtue, high-spirited perhaps, but noble in his sensuous existence, and she had married him before all the world as an act of faith and conviction. But now, furious in her disillusionment, she regards his sneaking dishonesty as personally humiliating—how could she have been so blind?—and "rigid with bitterness and indignation" she waits for him to come home from his shift at the mine. She

---

[27] D.H. Lawrence, *Sons and Lovers*, p. 11.

has no intention of making a scene with her husband at this time (Inspectors are sometimes reluctant to confront their loved ones openly with their grievances), but Lawrence tells us that, ominously, "her manner had changed towards him." And thus when Walter enters the house, Gertrude tastes her gall and (much like Rose Sayer) greets him coldly and silently. "She was her father now," Lawrence observes, and "something in her proud, honourable soul had crystallised out hard as rock."

Make no mistake, Gertrude intends to punish Walter for his sins, but not briefly—not once, and then all is forgiven—and in a sad, twisted way her outrage roots itself deep inside her very conception of their relationship. From that day forward, Gertrude commits herself to a remorseless Pygmalion project with her husband, grimly determined to humiliate his Performer's carefree nature, and to force him to grow up and shoulder his share of Guardian burdens. Lawrence describes her undertaking with astonishing clarity, born out of his intimate observation of his own parents:

> She fought to make him undertake his own responsibilities, to make him fulfil his obligations. But he was too different from her. His nature was purely sensuous, and she strove to make him moral, religious. She tried to force him to face things.[28]

Gertrude settles on various methods of "re-forming" Walter over the next few years, though they all in some way

---

[28] D.H. Lawrence, *Sons and Lovers*, p. 14.

demand that he ask forgiveness for his Artisan nature. Sometimes she resumes her cold silence: she goes "about her work with closed mouth and very quiet," and Walter slinks away, "rather subdued, afraid to seem too jubilant in presence of his wife." At other times Lawrence describes how she "scathed him with her satire." Once, for example, when Morel comes home slighty tipsy, Gertrude admonishes him for his free-spending *and* his drinking: "There's money to bezzle [guzzle] with," she comments dryly, "if there's money for nothing else." But most often, infuriated to "battle-pitch," Gertrude clenches her fists and scolds him mercilessly, trying to shame him into acting more responsibly: "you, the most despicable liar that ever walked," she rages, "the house is filthy with you."

Gertrude tries to break Walter in one other way, as well, and I suspect that many Guardian women in difficult marriages follow a similar course of action. Female Guardians devote themselves conscientiously to their role as mother, and in an unsatisfying marriage, devoid of "finer intimacies," her relationship with her children can become her life's salvation. And thus, as Gertrude's children come along, conceived in lulls in the fighting with Morel, she transfers her love inexorably away from her husband. Her first son William, for example,

> came just when her own bitterness of disillusion was hardest to bear; when her faith in life was shaken, and her soul felt dreary and lonely....At last Mrs. Morel...turned to the child; she turned from the father.[29]

---

[29] D.H. Lawrence, *Sons and Lovers*, p. 14.

Gertrude makes much of the child—she "loved him passionately," Lawrence tells us—and whether intentionally or not, she makes Morel wildly jealous with her ardent preference for the boy. But besides compensating for her disappointment, Gertrude also holds her sons up as a reproach to her husband. In the midst of one argument, when Walter drunkenly orders her to leave his house, she denies him his crude victory by scorning him as unfit to raise his own children:

> "No," she cried loudly, "you shan't have it *all* your own way; you shan't do *all* you like. I've got these children to see to. My word," she laughed, "I would look well to leave them to you."[30]

I want to make clear that few Guardian women are this possessive, or this manipulative, with their children. Indeed, Lawrence's main purpose in *Sons and Lovers* is to dramatize how Gertrude's obsession with her sons is indeed *ab*normal, tragically interfering both with her growth in her marriage and their growth into independent manhood.[31] Nor do I want to leave the impression that Gertrude—as the Guardian—is all to blame for this frightening turn in her marriage. Morel the Artisan is just as responsible. "She would have felt sorry for him," Lawrence admits, "if he had once said, 'Wife, I'm sorry.' But no; he insisted to himself that it was her fault." Lawrence is thus very clear that the

---

[30] D.H. Lawrence, *Sons and Lovers*, p. 23.

[31] Lawrence's understanding of the debilitating effect of Guardian mothering compares impressively with David Levy's clinical analysis in his book, *Maternal Overprotection* (New York, 1966).

Morels' marriage is "a battle between the husband and wife," which is his way of saying that the fault lies in the dynamics of this *relationship*. It is an Inspector-Performer problem, with all too much blame on both sides.

To be sure, as I detailed in *Volume One,* Walter responds to Gertrude's nagging and belittling with a brutal Pygmalion project of his own. Driven "out of his mind" by Gertrude's contempt, he tries to beat down his wife's superiority by behaving even *more* irresponsibly than before. He begins drinking heavily again, and he attempts to avenge himself (blustering with his beer) by striking back at his wife with violent threats and physical abuse. His behavior falls at times into a classic Artisan pattern of violence and shame and redoubled violence. Lawrence describes how, after one particularly stormy fight, "Walter was for some days abashed and ashamed, but he soon regained his old bullying indifference"; and another night, after sending Gertrude reeling with a blow, Morel sobers up a bit and confesses he dreads his wife: "Having hurt her, he hated her."

Walter's violent reprisals, of course, only strenghten Gertrude in her resolve to defeat this wicked man and bring him to righteousness. He might drink himself into a rage and bloody her brow, but his violence never really touches her hard Coppard core:

> She still had her high moral sense, inherited from generations of Puritans. It was now a religious instinct, and she was almost a fanatic with him, because she loved him, or had loved him. If

he sinned, she tortured him. If he drank and lied... she wielded the lash unmercifully.[32]

The terrible irony is that both Gertrude's Pygmalion project to lift Walter from sin, as *well* as Walter's reciprocal Pygmalion project to get her off his back, have exactly the opposite effect on each other. Lawrence understood intuitively what modern social-field psychology has clearly demonstrated, that resistance to change seems to operate on a stubborn principle of contradiction, force met with counterforce.[33] And thus, instead of changing (or "improving") each other's nature in any essential way, Gertrude and Walter's interpersonal battering actually galvanizes each other's temperament, and their marriage becomes a series of self-perpetuating, escalating rounds of conflict[34]—a "fearful, bloody battle," as Lawrence puts it, "that ended only with the death of one."

It is fair to say, however, that Gertrude is the more dogged Pygmalion, and that she survives the infighting far better in the long run. Although Lawrence describes the Morels' marriage as "this deadlock of passion between them," he concedes that, as a tough-minded Inspector Guardian,

---

[32] D.H. Lawrence, *Sons and Lovers*, p. 16.

[33] See Watzlawick, Weakland, and Fisch's discussion of their clients' resistance in *Change: Principles of Problem Formation and Problem Resolution* (New York, 1974), pp. 103-109, and pp. 133-140.

[34] Social-field theorists have labeled such an inescapable tug of war as "The Game Without End." See Watzlawick, Beavin, and Jackson's *Pragmatics of Human Communication* (New York, 1967), pp. 232-236.

Gertrude "was the stronger." Gertrude might never be able
to punish Walter into the sober, dutiful Guardian husband
she had intended, but her tenacious assault and his alcoholic
revenge do finally break his strength, and he inevitably
relinquishes his place to his sons, living out the rest of his
life as "more or less a husk," drained of his pride and
vitality. Gertrude's victory is thus pyrrhic, won at the
horrible cost of her own happiness, and Lawrence describes
the tragedy of her Pygmalion project-gone-mad with
precision, but also perhaps with a touch of compassion:

> The pity was, she was too much his opposite. She could not be
> content with the little he might be; she would have him the
> much that he ought to be. So, in seeking to make him nobler
> than he could be, she destroyed him.[35]

Sir Peter Teazle

The male Inspector Guardian is less common in literature
than the female, and in some instances less harshly
portrayed. While he is often stereotyped as a miserly, lonely
old man such as Silas Marner or Ebenezer Scrooge, these
characters usually redeem themselves by the end of their
stories, discovering before it is too late the value of a
generous heart. However, when the Inspector is a younger
man, and thus more interested in marriage—and Pygmalion
projects—literature reverts to type and depicts him just as
cruelly as it does the female. The male Inspector-in-love is
almost always a pinched and sour young man, Master Blifil

---

[35] D.H. Lawrence, *Sons and Lovers*, p. 16.

in Henry Fielding's *Tom Jones*, for example, or the aptly named Cecil "Vyse" in *A Room with a View*, whom E.M. Forster describes as impeccably austere:

> [Cecil] was mediæval. Like a Gothic statue. Tall and refined, with shoulders that seemed braced by an effort of will, and a head that was tilted a little higher than the usual level of vision, he resembled those fastidious saints who guard the portals of a French cathedral.[36]

Of course, both stereotypes—the old skinflint and the young prig—do an injustice to the male Inspector Guardian, exaggerating his precise, painstaking nature out of all proportion. But one character who offers us a more gently comical view of the Inspector is Sir Peter Teazle in Richard Brinsley Sheridan's eighteenth century comedy of manners, *The School for Scandal*. Sir Peter is both a stingy old man and an ill-used "new" husband in this sparkling play, and yet he overcomes both stereotypes to win his lady's heart, as well as the affection of the audience.

"When an old bachelor marries a young wife, what is he to expect?" Thus begins Sir Peter's first woeful speech in the play, though the question might better be framed as: What should an old Inspector Guardian expect when he marries a young Performer Artisan? Sir Peter is a stern and frugal old Londoner of considerable fortune, a confirmed bachelor at fifty who finally ventured matrimony when he found what he believed was a properly chaste and modest wife. "I

---

[36] E.M. Forster, *A Room with a View* (Vintage ed.), pp. 99-100.

chose with caution," he explains, "—a girl bred wholly in the country, who never knew luxury beyond one silk gown, nor dissipation above the annual gala of a race ball." Sir Peter (his surname "Teazle" is clearly satirical) courted this simple country girl, strolling with her under the elms on her father's farm, telling her stories of his gallant youth, chucking her "under the chin" like a rich uncle. The pretty-figured girl was "kind and attentive" to Sir Peter, and though privately she thought him a "stiff, peevish old bachelor," she coyly waited until their wedding-day to voice her criticism, as Sir Peter mournfully recalls:

> We tift a little going to church and fairly quarrelled before the bells had done ringing. I was more than once nearly choked with gall during the honeymoon, and had lost all comfort in life before my friends had done wishing me joy.[37]

Indeed, once introduced to London society, Lady Teazle (the name "Teazle" fits *her* quite well) shamelessly defied her husband and gave full play to her Performer's nature, gayly taking up with the most scandal-loving set in the wicked city, led by wags and gossips such as "Sir Benjamin Backbite" and "Lady Sneerwell." And thus, as the play opens, Sir Peter has been seething for six months, met "with nothing but crosses and vexations" in his marriage, watching in embarrassment and outrage as his impetuous young wife "plays her part in all the extravagant fopperies of fashion and the town."

---

[37] Richard Brinsley Sheridan, *The School for Scandal*, ed. C.J.L. Prince (London, 1971), I,ii,5-9. All quotations are from this edition.

This is not to say that Sir Peter has meekly acquiesced in his lady's folly. Inspectors rarely overlook the opportunity for a Pygmalion project, and Sir Peter almost daily admonishes his wife for her carefree and unauthorized Artisan spending:

> Lady Teazle, Lady Teazle, I'll not bear it!...tho' my life may be made unhappy by your temper, I'll not be ruined by your extravagance!...you shall throw away no more sums on such unmeaning luxury.[38]

Lady Teazle holds her ground with a gentle mockery:

> Sir Peter, Sir Peter, you may bear it or not as you please; but I [will] have my own way in everything....Why will you endeavor to make yourself so disagreeable to me and thwart me in every little elegant expense?....I'm sure I'm no more extravagant than a woman of fashion ought to be.[39]

Sir Peter attempts to assert himself and commands his wife to accept the deprivations of winter, strictly forbidding her to fill her dressing-room with anything so frivolous (and expensive) as "greenhouse flowers." But Lady Teazle cheerfully retorts that *she* mustn't be blamed for the cold weather. "I wish it was spring all the year round," she assures him like a true Dionysian, "and that roses grew under one's feet!"

---

[38] Richard Brinsley Sheridan, *The School for Scandal*, II,i,1,14-15,18-19. Note that Sir Peter builds to a role-directive style of communication: "You shall throw away no more...."

[39] Richard Brinsley Sheridan, *The School for Scandal*, II,i,2-4.16-17,77-78. Note Lady Teazle's very clearly role-informative style of communication: "I will have...Why will you?...I'm no more...."

Sir Peter shifts tactics and in good Guardian fashion tries to establish his traditional rights: "Very well, Ma'am, very well; so a husband is to have no influence, no authority?" But Lady Teazle merrily dismisses the idea, making sure she teases her husband about his age: "Authority! no, to be sure—if you wanted authority over me, you should have adopted me and not married me." Stung by the truth, Sir Peter next appeals to her sense of personal obligation. "What have I not done for you?" he reminds her:

> I have made you a woman of fashion, of fortune, of rank—in short, I have made you my wife... what had you to do with the fashion before you married me?[40]

Lady Teazle, however, finds less reason for gratitude or obedience in her husband's petition than justification for her stylish social life. "For my part," she counters, "I should think you would like to have your wife thought a woman of taste." And Sir Peter disastrously bungles his entire argument attempting to drive home his point. "Zounds! Madam," he assures her, "you had no taste when you married *me*!" Sir Peter's blunder is rather typical of him ("Was ever man so crossed as I am," he pleads, "everything conspiring to fret me!"), but it effectively concludes his debate with his wife, or what she calls their "daily jangle." Lady Teazle laughs and flies off to a party, and Sir Peter— Pygmalion bound—is left to stew in his own frustration.

---

[40] Richard Brinsley Sheridan, *The School for Scandal*, II,i, 64-66, 83-84.

To his credit, Sheridan was not content to leave Sir Peter as this cross, tight-fisted, bumbling stereotype. Sheridan's observation of human temperament was quite sophisticated, and he rounded his portrait of the Inspector Guardian considerably, adding the brilliant facets that were typical of all his characterizations, and that sets *The School for Scandal* above most other eighteenth century comedies.

First of all, as I have suggested, Guardians spin out their lives in cycles of guilt and self-punishment, and Sir Peter insists on taking arduous responsibility for his miserable lot, insisting again that "when an old bachelor marries a young wife, he deserves—no—the crime carries the punishment along with it." On the other hand, for all his avowed disappointment with his "helpmate," as he sarcastically refers to Lady Teazle, Sir Peter seems at times rather to enjoy her taunts and barbs. Inspectors can be strangely pleased by interpersonal conflict, as if needing some sort of disagreement to exercise their severity, and Sir Peter clearly admires his wife's impertinence:

> Yet with what a charming air she contradicts everything I say, and how pleasingly she shows her contempt for my authority! Well, tho' I can't make her love me, there is great satisfaction in quarrelling with her, and I think she never appears to such advantage as when she's doing everything in her power to plague me.[41]

Inspectors are also drawn to Artisans for their impudent sexuality, so in contrast to their own ingrained puritanism, and certainly Sir Peter derives a good deal of sexual excitement in quarrelling with his young wife. Sheridan

---

[41] Richard Brinsley Sheridan, *The School for Scandal*, II,i,121-127.

even points out that, in the heat of argument, Sir Peter is not above bribing Lady Teazle for a kiss. "There's nothing I could refuse you," he promises her in one scene, coaxing her amorously—"but seal me a bond for the repayment." However, Sir Peter's choice of metaphor, which likens his wife's embrace to a note of mortgage, reveals just how awkward and businesslike he is about expressing his physical passion, a problem characteristic of the Inspector, of all the Guardians for that matter.

Sir Peter might be sexually solicitous, but Sheridan suggests that he has a surprisingly shy and gentle side as well. Indeed, almost as soon as he introduces Sir Peter in the play, Sheridan begins to soften his character, offering glimpses of his heartfelt love for his young wife. Thus, Sir Peter complains to the audience in his opening monologue that Lady Teazle "dissipates my fortune, and contradicts all my humours," and yet he also confesses that "the worst of it is...I love her, or I should never bear all this." Though he mutters to his old servant Rowley about Lady Teazle's intolerable perverseness, the faithful Rowley knows his master too well and gently corrects him: "Come, come, Sir Peter, you love her, notwithstanding your tempers don't exactly agree." And Sir Peter even hopes (and this is quite touching) that he can somehow make himself jolly enough to please his wife: "How happy I should be," he sighs, "if I could tease her into loving me, tho' but a little!" Sheridan's point is certainly serious, and must not be lost amid the satire so often casually directed at the Inspector Guardians.

Beneath their severe, fastidious exterior lies a good-hearted and somewhat vulnerable type, earnestly wishing they could share in the Artisan's playful intimacy, but also sadly embarrassed by their lack of grace with the opposite sex.

Still, *The School for Scandal* is a comedy, perhaps the greatest comedy of the eighteenth century, and having carefully established Sir Peter's sympathetic side, Sheridan turns it skillfully into farce. Sir Peter himself protests to Rowley that he hates taking Lady Teazle to task. "I am myself the sweetest-tempered man alive," he insists—but then the punchline, "and so I tell her a hundred times a day." And in a later scene Sir Peter tries to persuade his wife to lay aside her contrariness and to appreciate his lovable nature. "Ah, Lady Teazle," he contends, "you might have the power to make me good humoured at all times." But Lady Teazle is willing to cease hostilities only if he admits her youthful superiority. "I'm sure I don't care how soon we leave off quarrelling, provided you'll own *you* were tired first." Sir Peter swallows hard at this challenge, but maintains his conciliatory tone. "Well—then let our future contest be, who shall be most obliging." Artisans are naturally cynical types, and Lady Teazle scoffs at her husband's naiveté, laughing "And never differ again!" Sir Peter grandly assures her, "No, never," but he simply cannot resist one last effort to gain the upper hand: "—tho' at the same time indeed, my dear Lady Teazle, you must watch your temper very narrowly; for in all our little quarrels—my dear—if you recollect, my love, you always began first."

Such determined amiability, of course, quickly erodes into full scale war. Sir Peter and Lady Teazle square off and accuse each other (in the *most* polite terms) of trying to start a quarrel, their exchanges punctuated with increasingly emphatic endearments—"my angel"..."my love"—until Sir Peter is beside himself with anger. "'Tis evident you never cared a pin for me," he finally declares, "and I was a madman to marry you—a pert, rural coquette," and working himself into a fury he vows that divorce is his only recourse. "I have done with you Madam!" he threatens her; "you are an unfeeling, ungrateful—but there's an end of everything." At first Lady Teazle answers in kind: "I was a fool to marry you—an old dangling bachelor." But Artisans are wonderfully practical types, and Lady Teazle quickly sees that this time she can gain advantage by *obliging* Sir Peter. So she calls her husband's bluff and quite cheerfully agrees to a separation, then runs off laughing, to let him boil in his anger: "Well, you are going to be in a passion I see, and I shall only interrupt you—so, bye! bye!" Inspector Guardians, on the other hand, take their anger earnestly, conscientiously, even moralistically, convinced that life's battles are no laughing matter. And thus Sir Peter curses his fate—"Plagues and tortures," he roars—but he is most galled by his wife's breezy good humor in the face of his rage:

> O, I am the miserablest fellow! But I'll not bear her presuming to keep her temper—no! she may break my heart, but she shan't keep her temper.[42]

---

[42] Richard Brinsley Sheridan, *The School for Scandal*, III,i,314-316.

After Sir Peter calms down and realizes how extravagant were his threats, he sets about making up with Lady Teazle in the most generous way he can imagine. Keirsey points out that "with all their seeming miserliness, still the [Inspectors] consider generosity the greatest of all virtues"[43]; and so, hoping "to remove all ground of quarrel" between them, Sir Peter quietly draws up two deeds of settlement, one giving Lady Teazle "eight hundred a year independent while I live," and the other leaving her "the bulk of my fortune at my death." Guardians hold instinctive regard for such official legal documents, particularly when money is being disposed of, and to make certain his drafts are properly constituted Sir Peter takes himself to the house of his sensible young friend, Joseph Surface, to ask his well-considered opinion.

Unfortunately, young "Surface" is a Promoter Artisan (an "ESTP"), a "smooth-tongue hypocrite" who has ingratiated himself with Sir Peter by mouthing the most noble sentiments, all the while energetically wooing every lady in sight, including Lady Teazle. Indeed, when Sir Peter enters Surface's library with his papers, Lady Teazle has just scrambled behind a folding screen in the room, having been very nearly caught in the young seducer's arms. Surface is barely able to avert disaster, listening effusively to Sir Peter's generous intentions for his wife, all the while steering him nervously away from the suspicious screen. But when Lady Teazle (huddled breathlessly on the other

---

[43] David Keirsey, *Portraits of Temperament*, p. 46.

side) overhears her husband's magnanimity, she is touched to the heart.

This famous "screen scene" is the hilarious climax of *The School for Scandal*, piling one amazing comic complication on top of another, but in the end the screen is thrown down, Lady Teazle is discovered, and she must face Sir Peter's stern interrogation. To his surprise, Lady Teazle offers no feeble, spur-of-the-moment explanation for her shocking conduct. She boldly denounces Surface and confesses the truth of their liason: "I came, seduced by his insidious arguments, at least to listen to his pretended passion." But she also swears that her husband's unselfish care for her welfare has changed her life. "Sir Peter," she concedes, "I do not expect you to credit me—"

> but the tenderness you expressed for me, when I am sure you could not think I was a witness to it, has penetrated to my heart and had I left the place without the shame of this discovery, my future life should have spoke the sincerity of my gratitude.[44]

With her conscience thus in crisis, Lady Teazle retires to Sir Peter's house, closes her doors to her circle of scurrilous friends, and waits as if in mourning for her husband's forgiveness.

We might question if Lady Teazle's sudden change of heart is altogether artless. After all, she is a Performer Artisan,

---

[44] Richard Brinsley Sheridan, *The School for Scandal*, IV,iii,501-506.

and thus quite accomplished at improvising her way out of tight spots—might candor have been her shrewdest ploy in such compromising circumstances? The play itself cleverly leaves the question open, for though at the very end Lady Teazle again disowns her London friends, returning with dramatic flourish their degree of "licentiate" from the school for scandal, she sounds dangerously unregenerate when she addresses the audience in the Epilogue:

> … was ever lively wife,
> Born with a genius for the highest life,
> Like me untimely blasted in her bloom,
> Like me condemned to such a dismal doom?[45]

Whatever the truth of Lady Teazle's new life, Sir Peter also undergoes a transformation in the play, only his is a good deal more convincing. As a rule, Guardians have some difficulty letting go of their grievances—remember that guilt is one of their favorite Pygmalion tools—and for some time Sir Peter is quite content to let his wife suffer in her sorrow. "Certainly a little mortification appears very becoming in a wife," he tells Rowley, and he believes "it will do her good to let her pine a little." Sir Peter was deeply impressed with Lady Teazle's confession, it is true, but for now he sees very little that is praiseworthy in her conduct. "We live in a damned wicked world," he has concluded, "and the fewer we praise the better."

---

[45] Richard Brinsley Sheridan, *The School for Scandal*, Epilogue, 15-18.

Rowley urges his master to go and comfort Lady Teazle, but Sir Peter is a social-minded Guardian, worried for his status, and he greatly fears the already growing London ridicule. If "it is known that we are reconciled," he despairs, "people will laugh at me ten times more." However, Rowley knows his master's heart and encourages him to "retort their malice only by showing them you are happy in spite of it." And so, finally, after seeing his young wife humbled and "in tears," Sir Peter understands his servant's wisdom: he must be generous with his love as well as with his money, and forgiveness is more important than reputation. He promises Rowley to turn a deaf ear to the scandal-mongers—"Efaith, so I will!"—and to begin anew with his repentant lady. "We may yet be the happiest couple in the country," he announces, though of course he qualifies his optimism with his Inspector's ever-lurking caution—"if I'm not mistaken."

*   *   *   *   *

Although Sir Peter and Lady Teazle appear to have found their way in *The School for Scandal*, this eccentric marriage of an "old bachelor" and a "young wife" might seem too improbable and contrived—too much the stuff of comedy— to offer much insight into human interaction. But let me suggest that virtually *all* Inspector-Performer relationships, all Guardian-Artisan relationships, for that matter, are in some sense such September-May affairs. By nature, the

Guardians seem eternally middle-aged or more, and the Artisans eternally childlike, and their happiness together, regardless of their difference in years, depends very much on their reaching some balance point between the prudence of age and extravagance of youth. This balance is not always easy to find, particularly for the Inspector Guardians, since they can be so firm in their sense of discipline and so persevering in their Pygmalion projects. In loving an Inspector, we must respect them for their sharp-eyed observation of rules and violations, even if they seem at times too strict in their duty and too critical of human weakness. For if Inspectors try perhaps too hard to impose what C.S. Forester calls their "economical soul" onto their loved ones, the evidence of literature suggests that, in most relationships, Inspectors have their humanities, and that they criticize neither cruelly nor selfishly, but out of a passionate concern for right-living and an unstinting loyalty to their marriage.

Chapter 5

The Supervisor

...marriage, though it may add some comforts to life, is in fact a very...difficult affair towards which in order to perform one's duty, that is, to lead a decorous life approved of by society, one must adopt a definite attitude just as towards one's official duties.

———Leo Tolstoy[1]

Of all the Guardians, the most outspoken Pygmalions are the Supervisors (Myers's "ESTJ's"). While the Inspectors ("ISTJ's") go about their Pygmalion projects with quiet determination, preferring to avoid open conflict, the more outgoing Supervisors seem innately poised for confrontation, and are quite comfortable, even at times self-satisfied, in energetically reprimanding their loved ones for their misconduct. This is not to say that Supervisors seek out interpersonal discord; on the contrary, like all the

---

[1] Leo Tolstoy, *The Death of Ivan Ilych and Other Stories*, trans. Aylmer Maude (Signet ed.,1960), p. 110.

Guardians, they expect cooperation in their marriages and their families. But Supervisors stubbornly believe that the smooth operation of any institution or community, including marriage and the family, depends to a large extent on all parties following the socially approved rules and procedures, and thus they do not hesitate, as Keirsey puts it, to "read the riot act to anyone who steps out of line... they feel obligated to do it."[2] This readiness to censure any and all improprieties makes the Supervisors our most faithful public watchdogs, it is true, but the evidence of literature suggests that, taken too far, such admirable vigilence can strain their more intimate relationships, stifling their loved ones at times in an atmosphere of accusation and nagging disapproval—and in extreme cases forcing the spouse into open revolt.

Torvald Helmer

In many of his later plays—the so-called "social dramas"— Henrik Ibsen entraps his Artisan or Idealist major characters in a nineteenth century social world that might well be called Guardian in its strict conventionality. This repressive society is not entirely evil in the plays, of course, and Ibsen often embodies its conservative Guardian (or "Victorian") values in a whole range of kindly, well-intentioned minor characters who want nothing more than to provide a dependable home for their loved ones. (See my discussion of Ibsen's *Hedda Gabler* in *Volume One, The*

---

2 David Keirsey, *Portraits of Temperament*, p. 52.

Artisan.) However, in his most well-known play, *A Doll House*, Ibsen chose a more dominating and somewhat less sympathetic character to represent the Guardian temperament: Torvald Helmer, a solid, upstanding Supervisor, who believes his career and his family are models of social decorum, prospering under his watchful eye; but who is finally shown the truth of his Pygmalion marriage by his wife Nora, in what is still perhaps the most powerful scene of personal rebellion in modern drama.

Torvald Helmer has been married eight years to his adorable Nora, and they live with their three apple-cheeked children in a "beautiful, happy home"—to all appearances the "doll house" of the play's title, although Ibsen rather dryly describes it as "tastefully but not expensively furnished." Helmer is a business and tax attorney, and he has devoted himself scrupulously to his profession, advocating a stern system of justice that would force the liars and cheaters ("degenerates" he calls them) into "openly confessing their crimes and taking their punishment." However, his income has been relatively uncertain because he is "physically revolted" by the immorality of such criminals, and has always refused to "touch any cases that aren't clean and decent." Despite the lost commissions, he is enormously proud that his "official career," as he puts it, is "above reproach," and indeed his high standards have finally profited him. Due to his fastidious reputation, he has recently been named manager in the local bank, a position that calls for all of his

Supervisor's grave decisiveness and faithful attention to detail. Helmer is to take up his duties right after the first of the year (*A Doll House* is set over Christmas week); and though he has decided to spend much of the holiday in his study, examining the bank's personnel and procedures—he intends "to have everything in order by New Year's"—he pauses briefly to appreciate his good fortune, articulating for us his unmistakeably Guardian notion of success: "Ah, it's so gratifying to know that one's gotten a safe, secure job, and with a comfortable salary."

While Torvald's prospects are certainly optimistic, his Guardian nature is to proceed cautiously, taking no good turn in life for granted. And thus when Nora comes home wanting to show off her Christmas shopping, he does not know quite what to make of her enthusiasm, nor of her unauthorized spending, and he pulls himself warily from his study to question her good sense:

> (*After a moment he opens the door and peers in, pen in hand.*)
> Bought, you say? All that there? Has the little spendthrift been out throwing money around again?[3]

Nora's spirits are too high this Christmas Eve to be brought to earth by her husband's half-teasing accusation, though she does fold her wings a bit, hoping to avert Torvald's censure by reminding him of their new prosperity. "Oh, but

---

[3] Henrik Ibsen, *A Doll House*, in *Ibsen: Four Major Plays*, trans. Rolfe Fjelde (Signet ed., 1965), p. 44. All quotations are from this translation.

Torvald," she urges him gently, "it's the first Christmas we
haven't had to economize." Nora even shyly suggests that,
if money is really so scarce, they might borrow against his
new salary to tide them over. Helmer (quite alarmed at the
thought) decides he must sharpen his censure and nip such
irresponsibility in the bud. He feels it is "his duty as man of
the house not to indulge [Nora] in whims and fancies," and
so he takes a moment to lecture his wife about one of the
Guardians' eternal concerns, the likelihood of unforeseen
disaster:

> Nora! (*Goes over and playfully takes her by the ear.*) Are
> your scatterbrains off again? What if today I borrowed a
> thousand crowns, and you squandered them over Christmas
> week, and then on New Year's Eve a roof tile fell on my head,
> and I lay there—[4]

Nora objects rather passionately that, in the event of such a
tragedy, something as heartless as a note of debt simply
"wouldn't matter," but the very idea of borrowing is repug-
nant to Torvald, violating sound economic principles, and
he feels he must put his foot down:

> Nora, Nora, how like a woman! No, but seriously, Nora, you
> know what I think about that. No debts! Never borrow![5]

Nora quickly droops and acquiesces—"Yes, whatever you
say, Torvald"—and her game of wounded compliance
works wonders with her husband. Like all the Guardians,

---

[4] Henrik Ibsen, *A Doll House*, p. 44.
[5] Henrik Ibsen, *A Doll House*, p. 44.

Supervisors expect their loved ones to follow their rules, not because they have been bullied into submission, but out of *respect* for the rules and the rightness of their authority. In other words, it is not enough that we simply obey their directives; Supervisors want us to obey of our own free will and for the right reasons—to see the correctness of their position and to agree with their criticism—and they are often taken aback when their discipline is not met with genuine gratitude.[6] Thus, in this case, Torvald is puzzled when he sees how downcast his admonitions have made Nora. She is obeying him, but not gladly or thankfully, and, fearing that perhaps he has been too harsh with his young wife, he decides he had better humor her:

> Come on, don't be a sulky squirrel. (*Taking out his wallet.*) Nora, guess what I have here.[7]

As I have said, no matter how close-fisted they are, Guardians hate to be thought of as miserly, and so Helmer (hoping to make up with Nora) insists that she take a few additional crowns for her Christmas expenses, and he coaxes her to think of something special for herself: "Tell me just what—within reason—you'd most like to have." Nora brightens considerably at Torvald's prudent benevolence and promises to be "sensible" about her purchases. "I save everything I can," she reminds her husband, but this timid assertion of her own capabilities only starts Helmer off again on his genial condescension:

---

[6] David Keirsey, *Portraits of Temperament*, p. 52.
[7] Henrik Ibsen, *A Doll House*, p. 45.

(*Laughing*). Yes, that's the truth. Everything you can. But that's nothing at all.... Exactly the way your father was. You're never at a loss for scaring up money; but the moment you have it, it runs right out through your fingers.[8]

At this point, in the midst of his firm but lighthearted scolding, Torvald spies evidence of another of what he considers Nora's hereditary dissipations: macaroons. Torvald has expressly forbidden his wife the little cakes— "he's afraid they'll ruin [her] teeth"—and when his eagle eye detects a crumb on her lip (has she weakened while out shopping and treated herself against his wishes?), he furrows his brow and puts her through a sterner inquisition. "Look me straight in the eye," he directs her:

(*Shaking an admonitory finger*). Surely my sweet tooth hasn't been running riot in town today, has she?... My sweet tooth really didn't make a little detour through the confectioners? ....Hasn't nibbled some pastry?....Not even munched a macaroon or two?[9]

Nora (lying) protests her innocence, and Helmer (lying as well) relaxes his severity, deciding not to press his cross-examination: "There, there now. Of course I'm only joking." Torvald's forbearance, however, is largely cosmetic, employed in good Victorian fashion to keep the façade of the marriage as decorous as possible. And though he manages to smooth over trouble in this first scene in *A Doll House*, his "charmed life" with Nora is already showing

---

[8] Henrik Ibsen, *A Doll House*, p. 46.
[9] Henrik Ibsen, *A Doll House*, p. 46.

signs of strain. Indeed, Torvald follows this pattern of scrutiny, accusation, and patronizing forgiveness throughout the rest of the play—it is the Supervisor's way—but it ends by wholly destroying Nora's love for him, and costing him his marriage.

Clearly, Torvald's Pygmalion project with Nora is an attempt to shape her into a dutiful, wholesome, and obedient Guardian wife and mother—the "Angel in the House," as one immensely popular nineteenth century poem defined the Victorian female.[10] Helmer observes all the precepts of the age and of his class. He expects Nora to serve her family, "to please us all...that's what counts." He requires her to live by the highest moral standards—"No false notes. (*Putting his arm about her waist.*) That's the way it should be, isn't it? Yes, I'm sure of it." And he takes it as a matter of course that she will, in all important decisions, loyally "give in to [her] husband's judgment."

On her side, bound as she is by the Victorian rules of marriage, Nora tries even against her own integrity to be Torvald's Guardian ideal, his little "squirrel," as he calls her. Thus, even though Nora presses at times (and nervously) to exert some small power in the relationship—"let's do as I say, Torvald"—most often she devotes herself tirelessly to her husband and children, wanting only "to keep up a beautiful, charming home—everything just the

---

[10] Walter E. Houghton, *The Victorian Frame of Mind* (New Haven, 1957), p. 341.

way Torvald likes it." Again, although Nora once weakly suggests that Helmer's excessive scruples are "such petty considerations," she usually seems in full agreement with her husband's meticulous morality. "I'm with [you] completely there," she assures Torvald in one scene, and in another she even asks him to instruct her in the proprieties: "Direct me. Teach me, the way you always have." And though Nora defies Torvald in little ways (with her chronic "untruths," such as the macaroons), she publically professes unquestioned obedience to his commandments. "You know," she assures her husband, "I could never think of going against you."

In this way, by obeying these Victorian laws of wifely conduct, Nora takes her proper place next to her husband in the marriage; they are "man and wife," as Torvald pictures them, adding his typical note of moral approval, "That's as it should be." But let me point out that Torvald's attitude toward Nora (much like Rose Sayer's toward Charlie Allnut) is also essentially parental. Helmer chides Nora in one scene for being a "Little Miss Willful," and he concedes another argument with paternal authority: "The child," he says, "can have her way." Nora admits that she is sometimes annoyed with Torvald's fatherlike efforts "to improve me," but most often she finds it wiser to play the helpless child-wife her husband prefers:

> NORA. You know, there isn't anyone who has your good
> taste—and I want so much to look well at the costume party.

> Torvald, couldn't you take over and decide what I should be
> and plan my costume?
> HELMER. Ah, is my stubborn little creature calling for a
> lifeguard?
> NORA. Yes, Torvald, I can't get anywhere without your
> help.[11]

Torvald is delighted to decide what character his wife will
be for this after-Christmas party (after all, he has been fashioning her to his liking all through their marriage), and his
choice of costume reveals another side of his expectations
for Nora, a curious second Pygmalion project that appears
to have been quite typical in Victorian marriages. Not only
does Torvald want his wife to be a dutiful and innocent
Guardian in her domestic habits (his "little squirrel"), but he
also wants to turn Nora, sexually at least, into a Performer
Artisan, a more playful and passionate creature he often
calls his "little songbird."[12] Thus, for her special role at the
party, he settles almost immediately on Nora's costume: she
will go, he announces, as his "capricious little Capri-girl"
and "dance the tarantella," a swirling, Dionysian folk-dance
she learned on their trip to southern Italy shortly after their
marriage.

---

[11] Henrik Ibsen, *A Doll House*, p. 69.

[12] In her novel *The Age of Innocence*, Edith Wharton calls this dual role
     for the Victorian wife a "miracle of fire and ice" (Scribner Library
     ed., p. 7). And John Fowles, speaking of the Dr. Jekyll and Mr.
     Hyde in all Victorians, generalizes the point in *The French
     Lieutenant's Woman*: "This—the fact that every Victorian had two
     minds—is the one piece of equipment we must always take with us
     on our travels back to the nineteenth century" (Signet ed., p. 288).

This is not to say that Torvald longs for a more Bohemian marriage, or that he wants Nora's performance at the party to "overstep the proprieties of art," as he puts it. Like many straightlaced Guardian husbands, Torvald occasionally dreams of a more impassioned relationship with his wife, and yet his conventionality is so deeply ingrained that real Dionysian fervor quite unnerves him. "Not so violent, Nora!" he orders her as she rehearses the tarantella a bit too evocatively; "No, no, that won't do at all." And even Torvald's fantasy life seems to reach back only to his first lawful sexual experience—his wedding night. He asks Nora,

> when [we're] out at a party, do you know why I talk to you so little and keep such a distance away; just send you a stolen look now and then—you know why I do it? It's because I'm imagining then that you're my secret darling, my secret bride-to-be....I pretend... that we're just coming from the wedding, that for the first time I'm bringing you into my house—that for the first time I'm alone with you—completely alone with you![13]

In many cases, as Keirsey has pointed out, Guardian romance centers on the courtship ritual and culminates in the first months of marriage,[14] with relations afterwards becoming more and more contractural, more a "service which is to be delivered by the female, performed dutifully and on request, presumably in return for social and

---

[13] Henrik Ibsen, *A Doll House*, p. 101.
[14] David Keirsey and Marilyn Bates, *Please Understand Me*, p. 84.

economic security."[15] To be sure, Torvald has adopted over the years this typically Victorian materialistic and proprietary attitude toward his wife. He buys Nora off (as we have seen) with Christmas money; he thinks of her as "my richest treasure," wanting to hoard her "all to himself"; and he is most displeased when she dares refuse his sexual advances—"What do you mean?...You will, won't you? Aren't I your husband?" However, even though Torvald has grown rather businesslike with Nora, he still remembers the passion of youth, and when he sees the opportunity to transform his wife for a night (and to recapture the sensuality of his honeymoon), he lets his fancy free and decides to turn Nora into the "enticing," "bewitchingly lovely" young Capri-girl he knew at the beginning of their marriage.

In this Artisan Pygmalion project, too, Nora does her best to please her husband. She has feared all through their marriage that if Torvald ever "stops enjoying my dancing and dressing up," she will lose all her influence with him. And so, paradoxically, to keep some measure of power in the relationship—some sense of personal significance—she feels she must again give Torvald what he wants and play the Capri-girl for him. At first, she tries to adapt her innocent "squirrel" routine to the role—"Your squirrel," she tells Torvald, "would scamper and do tricks"—but Nora is also perfectly capable of playing the more sensual Performer Artisan, invoking the power of Dionysus to meet

---

[15] David Keirsey and Marilyn Bates, *Please Understand Me*, p. 83.

her husband's needs. "Your lark would be singing high and low in every room," she assures him, even promising, "I'd be a wood nymph and dance for you in the moonlight."

Indeed, Nora performs her Artisan and Guardian roles so well in the marriage—"Is that my little lark twittering out there?" Torvald wonders, or "Is that my squirrel rummaging around?"—that it is difficult to tell exactly what her temperament *is* in the play. Is she a playful, childlike Artisan browbeaten into an obedient Guardian? Or is she a timid, innocent Guardian coerced into aping Artisan sensuality? However, near the end of *A Doll House*, late at night and after Nora's "overwhelming success" at the costume party, a terrible secret in her life comes to light, and the revelation shows us not only the extent of Torvald's tyranny in the marriage, but that Nora is neither an Artisan nor a Guardian at all. Rather, she is an Idealist (an "NF") repressed very nearly to the point of splitting into multiple personalities (see my *Pygmalion Project, Volume Three: The Idealist* for a full discussion of multiple personality), and struggling with her temperament's two essentially contradictory imperatives. First, she must maintain what Keirsey calls "sympathetic rapport"[16] with her husband, even if this means pretending to be someone she is not[17]; and second, she must search for her real identity.[18]

---

[16] David Keirsey, *Portraits of Temperament*, pp. 90, 102.

[17] Keirsey suggests the Idealists' characteristic propensity to defend themselves by means of splitting off into multiple personality: "The NF [Idealist] has an extraordinary capability to appear...to be whatever the beholder wants to see" (*Please Understand Me*, p. 63).

[18] David Keirsey, *Portraits of Temperament*, pp. 90, 101.

Nora's secret has shadowed her from the beginning of her marriage, but becomes an almost unbearable burden in the course of the play. We discover early in *A Doll House* that, some months after their wedding, Torvald fell dangerously ill, and would very likely not have survived another bitter northern winter. Nora, beside herself with worry, sought money for a trip to Italy from an underworld moneylender named Krogstad, but since women could not borrow without a man's consent at the time, she secured the loan by forging her father's name to the papers. Torvald soon regained his health in the warm south, and he and Nora returned to their doll house and to Torvald's impeccable career—only Nora, having learned how her husband despised borrowing money and bending the law, decided to keep the loan hidden from him, and to make the payments as best she could, out of her house money and whatever little piece-work she could find. Nora is actually quite proud of her courage and her sacrifice—it is the only significant independent action she has ever taken in her life—and she very nearly has the note payed off, when disaster strikes: Krogstad threatens to expose her unless she can persuade Torvald to make him his assistant at the bank. Nora pleads with her husband as we have seen in the play, begs him both as his squirrel and his lark, but Torvald is completely unyielding. And then late at night after the costume party, when he glances at his mail and discovers Krogstad's shocking letter of extortion, Torvald confronts Nora with all his Supervisor's puritanical outrage:

No more playacting. (*Locks the hall door.*) You stay right here and give me a reckoning....You understand what you've done? Answer! You understand? Oh, what an awful awakening! In all these eight years—she who was my pride and joy—a hypocrite, a liar—worse, worse—a criminal! How infinitely disgusting it all is! The shame!....I should have suspected something of the kind. I should have known....Be still! All your father's flimsy values have come out in you. No religion, no morals, no sense of duty—Oh, how I'm punished...you've wrecked all my happiness—ruined my whole future.[19]

Of all the Guardians, Supervisors are the most uncompromising defenders of social propriety, and indeed, even amid his overwhelming personal disgrace, Torvald's first thought is to keep up outward appearances:

The thing has to be hushed up at any cost. And as for you and me, it's got to seem like everything between us is just as it was—to the outside world, that is. You'll go right on living in this house, of course. But you can't be allowed to bring up the children; I don't dare trust you with them....From now on happiness doesn't matter; all that matters is saving the bits and pieces, the appearance—[20]

For days (indeed, all through the play) Nora has dreaded her exposure and has strained in near-hysteria to stave it off; but now as she witnesses her husband's innate capacity for selfishness and social hypocrisy, she begins to see her marriage and her life with a new clarity. When Torvald demands, "Can you see now what you've done to me?"

---

[19] Henrik Ibsen, *A Doll House*, p. 105.
[20] Henrik Ibsen, *A Doll House*, p. 106.

Nora's face hardens with comprehension and she answers icily, "Yes, I'm beginning to understand everything now."

This last, justly famous scene in *A Doll House* depicts Nora's awakening into an independent identity, but the casting off of years (no, centuries) of male domination is not an easy matter, and Ibsen almost at once tempts Nora to set aside her newborn self-awareness. As she and Torvald face one another, reevaluating each other in the light of this sobering disclosure, the front bell rings and the maid brings in a letter from Krogstad with the loan document attached; he has had a change of heart and now wishes only to forget the entire unfortunate incident. Torvald immediately rejoices: "Yes, yes, it's true. I'm saved. Nora, I'm saved!" And he just as quickly wants to put all the ugliness behind them, to return their relationship to its comfortable decorum: "No, we're not going to dwell on anything unpleasant...it's over now, it's over! You hear me Nora?"

Supervisors have an astonishing blind spot concerning the effect of their castigations on their loved ones. Supervisors somewhat naively believe, as Keirsey notes, "that, as long as he or she cares for the spouse and takes the proper responsibility for the spouse's health and welfare, the constructive 'lessons' which he or she offers the mate should not inhibit the other's affection."[21] And thus, in this scene, when Torvald realizes he is out of danger, he entirely disregards the cruelty of his previous accusations. He

---

[21] David Keirsey and Marilyn Bates, *Please Understand Me*, p. 84.

magnanimously forgives Nora her foolish woman's blundering, and fully expects to be forgiven by her:

> No, no—just lean on me; I'll guide you and teach you. I wouldn't be a man if this feminine helplessness didn't make you twice as attractive to me. You mustn't mind those sharp words I said—that was all in the first confusion of thinking my world had collapsed. I've forgiven you, Nora; I swear I've forgiven you.[22]

Nora, however, has seen too much to "just be grateful," as Torvald wishes, and she cannot simply forgive and forget. She responds with a frozen sarcasm, "My thanks for your forgiveness," and begins (with great symbolic meaning) to change out of her Capri-girl costume, while Helmer chatters on about the heartfelt satisfaction a husband takes in truly forgiving his wife:

> It's as if she belongs to him in two ways now: in a sense...she's become his wife and his child as well. From now on that's what you'll be to me—you little, bewildered, helpless thing. Don't be afraid of anything, Nora; just open your heart to me, and I'll be conscience and will to you both.[23]

From Krogstad's first hint of blackmail, Nora had expected (and desperately feared) that Torvald would miraculously step forward and protect her, taking all the responsibility for her "sin" onto his masculine shoulders. But now, as if a veil has fallen from her eyes, she sees that all her life she has been dependent on some man's strength and

---

[22] Henrik Ibsen, *A Doll House*, p. 107.
[23] Henrik Ibsen, *A Doll House*, p. 108.

indulgence, first her father's and then her husband's, and that she has virtually no sense of independent personality. "I went from Papa's hands into yours," she explains to a stunned Torvald, and she confesses with disgust, "I've lived by doing tricks for you....I've been your doll-wife here, just as at home I was Papa's doll-child." She believes that "It's a great sin what you and Papa did to me," and she realizes, finally, that she must free herself utterly from her husband's Pygmalion projects in order to learn for herself who she is. Keirsey describes the Idealists' "search for personal identity...for their 'true self'"[24] as the central purpose of their lives, and Nora calmly declares that she must begin this journey at once and alone:

> I have to try to educate myself. You can't help me with that....I have to stand completely alone, if I'm ever going to discover myself and the world out there. So I can't go on living with you.[25]

Supervisors, on the other hand, are so circumscribed by social convention, and so rarely question tradition or authority, that rebellious behavior in their spouses (or in their children) quite exasperates them, and calls forth all their most cherished defensive maneuvers. Torvald insists immediately that Nora must be out of her mind to think of leaving her home. "You're insane!" he cries, and demands, "What kind of madness is this?" But he also brandishes his legal power as her husband: "You've no right!" he blus-

---

ters—"I forbid you!" Then, when his attributions and his threats prove ineffective—"From here on," Nora informs him, "there's no use forbidding me anything"—Torvald tries to sting his wife's conscience with a series of pious accusations and condemning double-bind questions, a tour de force of Guardian guilt manipulation:

> Abandon your home, your husband, your children! And you're not even thinking what people will say...
>
> Oh, it's outrageous. So you'll run out like this on your most sacred vows... your duties to your husband and children?...
>
> Before all else, you're a wife and mother...
>
> Why can't you understand your place in your own home? On a point like that, isn't there one everlasting guide you can turn to? Where's your religion?...
>
> If religion can't move you, I can try to rouse your conscience. You do have some moral feeling? Or, tell me—has that gone too?[26]

Nora's insight is so lucid and so transfiguring in this scene, however, that she is able to brush aside Torvald's every appeal to social or religious duty with her quiet faith in her own self-discovery:

> I can't be concerned about that. I only know how essential this is...
>
> I have other duties equally sacred.... Duties to myself...
>
> I don't believe in that anymore. I believe that, before all else, I'm a human being, no less than you—or anyway, I ought to try and become one.[27]

---

[26] Henrik Ibsen, *A Doll House*, pp. 110-111.

[27] Henrik Ibsen, *A Doll House*, pp. 110-111.

With his every appeal thus countered by Nora's determined Idealism, Torvald slowly and begrudgingly leaves off his posturing and his psychological bullying. He acknowledges solemnly, shaking his head, "There's a gulf that's opened between us," but coercion is such second-nature to him that even his proposal to bridge their impasse is merely another Pygmalion project, not on Nora, this time, but on himself. "I have strength enough," he promises her, "to make myself over." In truth, Nora holds little hope that a Supervisor Guardian such as Torvald could ever put down Pygmalion's chisel long enough to make "our living together," as she envisions it, "a true marriage." Indeed, Nora is certain only that, whatever the cost, she must find her own way to the self she has never known. And so she gives Torvald back his wedding ring—"There has to be absolute freedom for us both," she insists—and in a final act of defiance that quite astounded Ibsen's complacent Victorian audiences, she throws her shawl about her shoulders and walks out into the winter's night, slamming her doll house door behind her.

Let me emphasize that, despite Ibsen's obvious sympathy with Nora's liberation, he does not portray Torvald as a villainous character in *A Doll House*. Torvald's attitudes and behavior, though overwrought at the end, are entirely in keeping with his Guardian temperament. From his own and from his era's perspective, he is very much the model of a benevolent, conscientious husband, molding and scolding his wife for her own good, as well as for the good of the family and society—or as Nora concedes, "I know the majority thinks you're right, Torvald, and many books agree with you, too." Trying to delineate Nora and Torvald's legitimate differences, Ibsen explained in his notes for *A Doll House* that there are "two kinds of conscience" in the play, one based on "natural feeling" and the other—"altogether different"—based on a "belief in authority."[28] And while Ibsen broadly characterized these two incompatible sensibilities as "feminine" and "masculine," Keirsey's more comprehensive analysis makes it clear that the tragic conflict in the play is between the Idealist and the Guardian temperaments, two ways of life that Ibsen firmly believed "do not understand each other."[29]

Sarah

In spite of its medieval-sounding title, Alan Ayckbourn's *The Norman Conquests* is a trilogy of comic plays about three contemporary English couples—two sisters and a brother and their significant others—who converge for a July weekend at "Mother's" run-down Victorian country house. First there is Annie, who lives a drab, patient life in the old place, caring for the invalid Mother, and who is visited regularly by her long-unannounced fiancé, a trusty though rather dim local Veterinarian named Tom. Next there is Annie's older sister Ruth, an efficient, skeptical,

---

[28] Henrik Ibsen, *From Ibsen's Workshop*, ed. William Archer, trans. A.G. Chater (New York, 1978), p. 91.

[29] Henrik Ibsen, *From Ibsen's Workshop*, ed. William Archer, trans. A.G. Chater (New York, 1978), p. 91.

and impossibly nearsighted businesswoman, and her husband Norman, a librarian and Lothario—a self-styled "three a day man"—who just wants to make all the women in his life happy. And last but fortunately not least there is Annie's and Ruth's older brother Reg, a tamed but still playful real estate agent (an "ISTP" Instrumentalist Artisan), and his wife Sarah—"Mother Doom" as Ruth calls her—a prim and domineering housewife, and one of the most accurately observed Supervisor Guardians I know of in literature.

Ayckbourn shuffles and deals these six characters into a series of the most wonderful sexual misadventures over the weekend, as Norman (a Sensualist Artisan—see *Volume One*) attempts to seduce Annie, Ruth, and Sarah in turn, all the while counselling Tom and Reg how to handle their women and their lives. But through all the interpersonal confusion in *The Norman Conquests*, all the quarrels and misalliances, Ayckbourn lets us glimpse one relatively stable, workable marriage: Sarah and Reg—a Guardian and an Artisan—a mutually irritating couple, to be sure, even at times belligerent in their Pygmalion projects, but each balancing the other in some satisfying way.

Ayckbourn wastes little time in the plays establishing Sarah's Pygmalion attitude toward her husband. Annie has asked Sarah and Reg down for the weekend so that she can steal away for a well-deserved holiday from Mother, and when Annie greets her in the opening scene, and innocently asks how Reg is, Sarah sadly confesses the truth:

Reg? [*Big sigh*] Oh well, he's still Reg you know. I've tried.
God knows I've tried but he'll always be basically Reg.[30]

Reg might not have shaped up very much under her
supervision, but Sarah has done her best, and she continues
to wear away at him on all fronts, even when Reg is not
present to benefit from the scolding. When Annie asks
about their drive down, Sarah complains, "Reg drove far
too fast as usual but we got here," and then continues
inconsistently with a breathless criticism of his usual
lethargy:

There are times when I think he's sleepwalking. I have to
force him to make an effort. Heaven knows how he runs a
business. I'd certainly never let him sell a house of mine.[31]

If Sarah seems slightly on edge and overcritical, she has
good reason. Although she assures Annie "oh, it's lovely to
come down," she lets drop that she has had a bad back of
late ("surely I wrote and told you? I'm sure I did. I was so
upset I wrote to everybody"), and her preparations for the
weekend were especially grueling:

We've had all the trouble of having to take the children to
their grandparents so that we wouldn't have to bring them
down here because we knew they would disturb Mother. I've
had all the trouble of delegating responsibility for the "Bring

---

[30] Alan Ayckbourn, *The Norman Conquests* (New York, 1975), p. 19.
All quotations are from this edition. Sarah's lament is a classic
statement of the interpersonal game that Eric Berne calls "Look
How Hard I've Tried" (*Games People Play* [Ballantine ed., 1964],
pp. 105-108).

[31] Alan Ayckbourn, *The Norman Conquests*, p. 19.

and Buy Sale" which I'm sure will be a disaster because I'm
the only one among them with any sort of organizing ability.[32]

Still, for all her sacrifice and her carefully reported aches
and pains, Sarah is looking forward to her weekend in the
country in one very sincere way. Supervisor Guardians
love to be entrusted with responsibilities, to prove
themselves reliable no matter how great the burden.
Keirsey believes this trustworthiness is the very "source of
their self-esteem,"[33] and Sarah seems almost eager to
assume the obligation of caring for Mother. Of course, she
will see to it that Reg does his part, whether he wants to or
not: "She's his mother. He can do something for her for a
change." But regardless of the interpersonal difficulties,
Sarah is more than willing to take charge of the whole
establishment. "Now, you're to leave everything to me,"
she directs Annie,

> I'm taking over. Just tell me what pills and potions Mother
> has and when she has them and then off you go.[34]

Reg is thus not the only member of the family to feel
Sarah's Pygmalion pressure over the weekend. Supervisors
will "take over" with anyone who appears to need the
discipline—as if filling a void of indecision—and Sarah
quickly sees that before she attends to Mother, her first
order of business is to smarten Annie up for her trip: "Now

---

[32] Alan Ayckbourn, *The Norman Conquests*, p. 26.

[33] David Keirsey, *Portraits of Temperament*, p. 46.

[34] Alan Ayckbourn, *The Norman Conquests*, p. 19.

then, how are you, let's look. Oh, Annie darling, you look just the same. Your hair...." Annie is an affectionate but rather scruffy and out of touch Idealist (an "INFP") who rarely thinks about her personal appearance. And though she assures Sarah contritely that she washed her hair just that morning, Sarah is not appeased, snapping, "What's the good of washing it if you don't brush it." And Annie's outfit? It's the same jumper she was wearing at the family gathering last Christmas, Sarah points out, sweetly, and she offers (sounding quite Pygmalion-like) "to chisel it off" her if she wants, and to buy her a new one.

Sarah happily assumes that Annie is off for the weekend with Tom, and she soon starts snooping and nudging about the progress of their relationship. "At Christmas," she confides, "we thought he was beginning to sit up and take notice of you just a little. Pricking up his ears." Annie resents the metaphor—"Like a mongrel with a pedigree bitch," she spits out—though she quickly remembers herself and asks Sarah politely to mind her own business: "Honestly, stop trying to pair us off." Supervisors hate to be caught in their meddling, and Sarah defends herself in a huff, observing that Annie has become "dreadfully coarse" living in the country. Annie holds her ground this time and rejoins that Sarah is "just a prude," a charge which clearly touches a nerve with Sarah, and which she simply cannot let stand unchallenged:

> No, I'm not a prude. No, I've never been called that. You can't call me a prude. That's not fair, Annie, I mean, I don't care for smutty talk or dirty jokes. I just don't find them

funny. Or particularly tasteful. But that isn't being a prude. That's normal decent behaviour which is something quite different.[35]

Hoping to convince Annie of her candor and her worldliness, Sarah presses Annie to tell her all about her rendezvous with Tom. Guardians love to gossip, as I have said, and Sarah is dying to know all the lurid details— "waking up in the morning," as she imagines it, "finding some exciting looking man beside you." And even though Sarah believes her rather wicked interest in Annie's "nice dirty weekend" proves she is no prude, her Supervisor's approval is nothing if not prudent:

> I think it's splendid. I think if you and Tom were to get away from this house, away from Mother and everything—it's the best thing you could do. It's what you both need. [*She kisses her.*] Very sensible.[36]

By this time, however, Annie's self-reproach and sense of the ridiculous in the conversation have gotten the better of her, and she nervously begins to spill out the truth of her weekend. She's not meeting Tom at all, she explains in guilty starts and stops, but her brother-in-law Norman, keeping a promise she made in his arms on the hearth rug last Christmas. Sarah is shocked almost speechless at the confession, and while Annie laughs uncontrollably in embarrassment (and relief), Sarah's Guardian mind immediately narrows into its stern, judgmental mode,

---

[35] Alan Ayckbourn, *The Norman Conquests*, p. 21.
[36] Alan Ayckbourn, *The Norman Conquests*, p. 22.

pausing only briefly to hammer into the open all the incriminating facts:

> SARAH: Rug?...Which rug?
> ANNIE: The brown nylon fur one in the lounge... [*She starts to giggle.*]...
> SARAH: Annie, pull yourself together... [*thumping the table*] Annie, what happened on the rug?
> ANNIE: Everything happened on the rug.
> SARAH: Does Ruth know?
> ANNIE: No.
> SARAH: Or Tom?
> ANNIE: No. [*Drying her eyes*] Oh dear....[37]

Supervisors determine guilt and innocence with unbelievable speed, as if breathing in and out, and Sarah makes her call on this disgraceful affair without any hesitation. "Well, I blame Norman," she decides; "this is absolutely typical...fur rug!" And then she turns her sanctimonious glare on Annie: "How could you even think of it?...I mean, I mean, you just don't go off on holiday with your sister's husband." The more agitated Sarah becomes, the more personal are her recriminations. "Did you think of Ruth?" she demands, "and Tom?" In any event, Sarah knows by now that her own weekend in the country, "away from it all," is in shambles, but she gathers her wits about her and announces her only responsible course. "I think it's just as well we are here," she informs Annie, as if reprimanding a naughty little girl, and with a curious sense of satisfaction in her voice,

---

[37] Alan Ayckbourn, *The Norman Conquests*, p. 24.

> You quite obviously need a rest. Now, I want you to sit down
> here and leave everything to me....And let's get this quite
> clear to start with. You are not going anywhere. Not while
> I'm in this house....Reg and I will cope. That's what we
> came down for. You can rest....That's final. You're staying
> here.[38]

Sarah, indeed, spends much of her time over the next two
days "coping" with (i.e. "coercing") one character after
another, as she tries to take control of this disastrous
weekend and make everyone in the family start behaving in
a decent, respectable manner. Norman is the first to feel
her wrath. When Tom wanders in from the garden and
mentions innocently that Norman is outside "generally
waving" his pyjamas about, Sarah (rattled by the
implications) hurries to intercept him, approaching Norman
with a glowering disapproval:

> I'm appalled at you, I really am....Annie of all people. How
> could you? What on earth made you do it?[39]

Norman, as I have said, is a puppyish, philandering
Sensualist Artisan, and he tries his best to explain about
Annie. As he sees it, last Christmas was "just festive fun,"
and this weekend was purely recreational: "Don't you see?
It would have been something different for her—exciting."
Norman also claims that he *loves* Annie, but Sarah
thoughtfully reminds him of his more serious commitments:
"Don't be ridiculous. You're married to Ruth." Norman

---

[38] Alan Ayckbourn, *The Norman Conquests*, p. 26.
[39] Alan Ayckbourn, *The Norman Conquests*, p. 96.

winces, "What's that got to do with it?" and wonders if Sarah has ever been fully in love:

> NORMAN: ...What do you say, Sarah? Would you say you were a fulfilled person?
> SARAH: I don't know what you mean.
> NORMAN: Are you happy then?
> SARAH: Yes—mostly. Occasionally. Now and then. I don't know. I don't have time to think about it. When you've a family like mine you're too busy—[40]

Preoccupied and often exhausted as they are with family responsibilities, Guardians certainly understand love and happiness far differently than Artisans, and when Norman flaunts his most loving traits—"I'm very warm and affectionate, you know"—Sarah maintains her conventional perspective: "Yes. So are dogs. But they don't make particularly good husbands." And when Norman tries again to describe the sensual freedom he wanted with Annie on their holiday—to "forget everything, everybody, just lie anonymously in each other's arms"—Sarah shakes her head sadly and reaffirms the inescapable Guardian social reality: "We'd still be here when you came back."

Sarah's most exasperating challenge over the weekend, however, is with what she regards as her own husband's moral indolence. Sarah requires Reg's help in keeping Annie and Norman under surveillance, but when she first orders Reg to spy for her—"Go and see if they're in

---

[40] Alan Ayckbourn, *The Norman Conquests*, p. 97.

there"—he refuses bluntly, as if well-practiced in countering such directives:

> Why don't you?....I'm not interested if they're in there. It doesn't matter to me if they're in there or not. You're the one who's interested if they're in there.[41]

No matter how often they are crossed in a relationship, Supervisors naturally assume that their orders will be carried out—after all, who's in charge?—and Sarah is quite put out at Reg's typical disobedience. "Will you please do as I ask for once," she seethes, and then, taking a deep breath (trying at least to remain in control of herself), she sighs:

> He's a difficult man. He is such a difficult man. Ask him to do a simple thing for you and there's a twenty minute argument.[42]

Reg, of course, has no idea why Sarah is so suspicious of Annie all of a sudden, and he suggests his wife calm down and let Annie be: "she's all right," he advises, "leave her alone." But Sarah knows her duty only too well. "Do you realize what would happen if I did?" she snaps, and then proceeds to explain archly to Reg about Annie and Norman's secret liason. As an Artisan, Reg is a mischievous type, full of fun, and he whoops with delight at the news, only to stifle his laughter under his wife's withering stare:

---

[41] Alan Ayckbourn, *The Norman Conquests*, p. 32.
[42] Alan Ayckbourn, *The Norman Conquests*, p. 33.

Frankly, Reg, I think there is something mentally wrong with you. I think you ought to see someone. I'm being serious.[43]

Guardians as a rule regard any act of independence on their spouses' (or their children's) part as bad, or even crazy, behavior,[44] and though Reg pleads for his own point of view—"I think it's funny, I can't help it"—Sarah quickly works herself into a bitter frenzy: "Yes, you can walk away but it's always left for me to deal with, isn't it?" Guardians are also expert at harboring their grievances ("gunnysacking" in Bernean terminology), then springing them punitively on their spouses in the heat of later, unrelated arguments, and Sarah now rattles off a list of Reg's transgressions:

> SARAH: It's left to me to explain why you walk straight upstairs as soon as anyone comes to visit us.
> REG: They're your friends.
> SARAH: It's me that's left looking stupid in front of the headmistress when you forget the names of your own children.
> REG: That was only once.[45]

Sarah has always been impatient with Reg's seclusive nature, often scolding him, "well...don't be too anti-social." But on his side, as a tool-loving Instrumentalist Artisan, Reg finds his greatest pleasure using his hands, making and mending things, and his beloved hobby since

---

[43] Alan Ayckbourn, *The Norman Conquests*, p. 35.

[44] Aaron Esterson, in his book *Leaves of Spring* (London, 1970), explores this point with great skill and subtlety, describing one family, for example, in which the daughter was seen as "mad and bad" by her clearly Guardian parents when she "was acting and experiencing most autonomously" (pp. 3-4).

[45] Alan Ayckbourn, *The Norman Conquests*, p. 35.

childhood has been building model airplanes and crafting little figures for his homemade table games. The mess annoys Sarah no end—"Our house is littered with little men," she grumbles—and now, incensed at his irresponsible sense of humor, she somehow equates his childlike amusement with family neglect:

> They run wild those children. You've done nothing for them. Nothing at all. If I didn't get them food, they'd starve, if I didn't buy them clothes, they'd be naked—you sit in that room, which I spend my whole life trying to keep tidy, fiddling with aeroplanes and bits of cardboard and now you can't be bothered with your own sister—[46]

Reg has finally heard enough, and tries to end the argument, gently at first, but with his own anger at last erupting:

> REG: Sarah please, would you kindly stop talking
> SARAH: No, I will not stop talking.
> REG: You have talked at me since I got up this morning— you have talked at me over breakfast—
> SARAH: It happens to be the only way I can get through to you—
> REG: You talked solidly in the car for an hour—nearly causing us to have a very serious accident...
> SARAH: Which was entirely your fault.
> REG: And ever since we've been here, you haven't stopped for a second. Now, for the love of God, shut up.[47]

Sarah's nerves break at this unconscionable abuse. "I will not be spoken to like that," she warns shakily, dissolving in

---

[46] Alan Ayckbourn, *The Norman Conquests*, p. 35.
[47] Alan Ayckbourn, *The Norman Conquests*, pp. 35-36.

tears; "Just who do you think it is you're talking to?" And when Reg answers in disgust, "I think, like you, I'm talking to a brick wall," he expresses quite clearly the essential futility of Pygmalion projects in "getting through" to a spouse and shaping a marriage.

Reg's attitude toward marriage and family life—and toward Sarah in particular—is more accurately described as "easygoing" and "accepting" than "indifferent" or "careless," as Sarah would have it. To be sure, Reg has his regrets about marrying Sarah. He jokes to Norman that, as a form of suicide, marriage is "slow and messy," and when he comes down to the country he is flooded with memories of a simpler, more private childhood. "When I sit here in this house and listen to the quiet," he muses,

> I wonder why I left. I had my own room here, you know. All my books, my own desk, a shelf for my hobbies. I'd sit up there in my school holidays...happy as a sandboy. I'd make these balsa wood aeroplanes. Dozens of them. Very satisfying.[48]

And Reg also has more intimate disappointments. When he first discovers Norman lingering with his overnight bag outside in the garden, Reg teases him enviously about his notorious womanizing. "Something lined up?" he winks at Norman; "Bit of stuff?....Lucky chap. Hasn't got a friend has she?" But when Norman seems to take him seriously, Reg quickly backs away: "I was only joking. I would

---

[48] Alan Ayckbourn, *The Norman Conquests*, p. 31.

never....Don't believe in that personally." Not all Artisans are as singlemindedly lecherous as Norman, of course, and Reg has committed himself quite conscientiously to his marriage, though lurking behind his good-natured banter with Norman are the clear signs of his boredom with Sarah, as he awkwardly confesses:

> Mind you, I've been tempted. When you've been married a few years...you can't help window shopping. You know, the old urge. But you keep it under control, don't you? You have to. Well, you may not have to. But I have to. Not that there isn't something to be said for it. I've often thought it might actually help a marriage sometimes. It gets a bit stale between you, you know....Perhaps if she—went off for a few days with someone—she might—well, it might make her a bit more...you know, give her a fresh...get her going again, for God's sake. If you follow me.[49]

"Ah," Norman answers with mock-sincerity (for he has just been given an idea), and Reg rather glumly concedes that all his own talking is nonsense:

> Mind you, it'd never work for us. Sarah would never dream of going off. Pity. If she did, I could. But we're not like you and Ruth, you see....And another thing. We've got children. You haven't. That makes a difference. Can't go gallivanting off—not with children. Responsibilities. Blast it.[50]

However, instead of dwelling on his disappointments and retaliating with a Pygmalion project of his own, Reg has learned through the years to make the best of his marriage, and to appreciate Sarah for her Supervisor's strengths.

---

[49] Alan Ayckbourn, *The Norman Conquests*, p. 177-178.
[50] Alan Ayckbourn, *The Norman Conquests*, p. 178-179.

Thus, he encourages Tom to see that marriage has its points: "I mean, there are compensations. Children—sometimes. Even Sarah—sometimes." And he defends Sarah to his sister Ruth, a Fieldmarshal Rational (an "ENTJ") who simply cannot understand why he married her. While he agrees with Ruth that he and Sarah "certainly have differences," Reg insists they are not "altogether incompatible," and he points out that his wife is "pretty good with the children. On her good days," and that she "runs the house very well. Better than you or Annie would. Or Mother." Artisans in general are relaxed and optimistic in their relationships, often just what a Guardian needs, and Reg doesn't ask for perfection in a mate. "Six of one..." is his philosophy, adding "It works out all right" with Sarah, "most days."

Reg values Sarah in one other way, as well, and his explanation reveals wonderful insight on Ayckbourn's part into the dynamics of the Guardian-Artisan marriage. Ruth makes fun of Reg for "running round in circles" for Sarah, but Reg will not complain. He knows his own lackadaisacal nature well enough that he depends on Sarah's unfailing supervision virtually to propel him through his life. "That's all right," he tells Ruth, "I don't mind":

> I prefer being told what to do really. I often think if nobody told me what to do I'd never do any thing at all. I remember [Sarah] went away once for a fortnight. When her father was ill. Took the children with her. Left me on my own in the house. Do you know I felt myself gradually slowing down. At the end of ten days I was hardly moving at all.

> Extraordinary. It was as if she'd wound me up before she left and now I was running down.[51]

As an Artisan, Reg might battle against Sarah's manipulation, and have his regrets about her bossiness, but he always prefers to look on the bright side, and—like many Artisans with Guardian spouses—he feels happily balanced by the energy and the discipline Sarah infuses into his life.

However, this "sordid weekend" has tilted Sarah and Reg's balance somewhat, and has them dangerously at each other's throats. Sarah ends their argument in the dining room with uncharacteristic violence, by throwing a tin of water biscuits at Reg and sobbing, "You're contemptible....God knows what's going to happen to us"— though *Reg* certainly knows he's in for a lengthy stretch of grim Guardian browbeating. Again voicing Ayckbourn's remarkable understanding of Artisans and Guardians, Reg explains to Norman (who is even more seriously in Sarah's bad books), that his wife has "a long memory" for recriminations:

> You'll be told when you're forgiven and not before. She doesn't talk to me for days on end sometimes. Amazing how she remembers to keep it up. I mean, if I have a row in the morning, when I come home in the evening I've forgotten all about it. Until I open the front door. Then it hits you

---

[51] Alan Ayckbourn, *The Norman Conquests*, p. 130.

straightaway. Atmosphere like a rolling pin. Know what I
mean? She's got great emotional stamina, my wife.[52]

Norman certainly had a memorable Saturday night, getting
disgustingly drunk on homemade wine, attacking Mother—
even making a wobbly pass at Sarah—and, indeed, Sarah
tries to bludgeon him into shape at breakfast Sunday
morning with her infamous silent treatment. "Nobody in
this house," she hisses at him, "is speaking to you ever
again." But by dinner, and in a surprising shift of tactics,
Sarah has decided to try to make Norman behave himself
by pleading her debility. Wanting the family simply to sit
down together for a "civilized meal," Sarah entreats
Norman to restrain himself—"Will you try, just for this
evening, not to start any more scenes?"—and then she
solemnly explains the consequences if he does not "make
an effort":

> I don't know if you've realized it, Norman, but I have had a lot
> of nervous trouble in the past. And every time I come down
> here, I have a relapse. When I get home from this house, I
> find I'm shaking all over. For days. And I get these rashes up
> the insides of my arms....Now it's not fair on me, Norman. I
> have a family to look after, a house to run.[53]

---

[52] Alan Ayckbourn, *The Norman Conquests*, p. 148.

[53] Alan Ayckbourn, *The Norman Conquests*, p. 58. Sarah's comment
about her rash flaring up brings to mind again Franz Alexander's
work on psychosomatic illness. Alexander and French's *Studies in
Psychosomatic Medicine* (New York, 1948) includes two papers that
suggest a clear connection between the Monitor Guardian
temperament and skin disease. Milton L. Miller argues in "A
Psychological Study of a Case of Eczema and a Case of Neuroder-
matitis," that "certain emotional characteristics appear to stand out
as common for this type: retarded psychosexual development,

Norman promises, with true Artisan spontaneity, to do all he can to make the evening a success: "Make it a banquet, Sarah my love." And then, when Sarah corrects him uneasily that there's no food in the house, he continues confidently: "We can improvise. What do we need?" What Sarah really needs from Norman, however, is quiet obedience, not festivity, nor even help with the preparations. "Yes, all right Norman, I'll do it," she insists, explaining further that "if there's too much noise I get these headaches."[54]

Sarah has also changed tactics with Reg by this time, and she appeals to him as well for cooperation—"I want us to have a quiet meal...to behave in a civilized manner"—though with her husband she dispenses with her polite manners and opens with a deadly threat: "I'll never forgive you if you don't try. I mean it, Reg." But Sarah cannot resist another play for sympathy, and so starts up what appears to be a quite familiar interpersonal extortion:

SARAH: ...Well, any more of this and you know what'll happen? What always happens when I come down here.

---

tension, guilt, anxiety"(p. 405), and he characterizes them as a "ceaselessly active, precocious, assertive, egocentric"(p. 403) personality. And in "The Emotional Settings of Some Attacks of Urticaria," Leon J. Saul and Clarence Bernstein, Jr. very nearly describe Sarah's own interpersonal predicament in one of their patients: "The onset occurred when the patient felt on the verge of frustration in all her human relations"(p. 438).

[54] Franz Alexander notes in his book *Psychosomatic Medicine* (New York, 1950), that "the literature abounds with reports that fatigue and emotional stress...may bring about headaches" (p. 155).

REG: Oh no? You've not got the shakes again, have you?
SARAH: You ought to know me by now, Reg. I can't bear these sorts of atmospheres.
REG: It's not your back, is it?
SARAH: Not at the moment. But the way I've had to run around trying to cope with one crisis after another....
REG: Well, sit down. Have a rest for a second.
SARAH: [*snapping*] How can I sit down? Be sensible. How can I possibly sit down?[55]

Inevitably, and even though Sarah thinks she has the evening safely organized, the forces of chaos begin to mount against her. First of all, when dinner is ready, Sarah attempts to direct everyone else to his or her proper seat at the table, appropriate boy next to appropriate girl. "Let's get seated," she announces officiously; "Reg, you go up at the end, would you?...no, not there, Ruth dear. Would you mind sitting one seat further up?....You're here, Tom. Sit here." In the wandering and muttering that ensue, Reg graciously offers his seat to Annie, but Sarah holds on politely: "No, she can't sit there. She's out of order." And the exercise quickly turns into mass confusion, with everyone (everyone except Ruth, that is) shuffling back and forth

---

[55] Alan Ayckbourn, *The Norman Conquests*, pp. 60-61. Again, Alexander and French, in *Studies in Psychosomatic Medicine* (New York, 1948), cite two studies that shed some light on Sarah's ailments. Leon Saul points out that, in a certain (and clearly Guardian) type of person, "repressed rage" seems the cause of their back pain ("A Clinical Note on a Mechanism of Psychogenic Back Pain," p. 545). And J.L. Fetterman suggests quite brilliantly that the localization of psychosomatic pain in the back may have to do with the (typically Guardian) patient's upright posture, "implying adulthood with all its responsibilities and exertions" ("Vertebral Neuroses," p. 545).

to accomodate everyone else—all punctuated by Sarah's more and more agitated pleas: "Why don't you leave it to me?....Why won't you listen? ....*[screaming]* Reg, will you kindly leave this to me." Sarah's shrieking finally penetrates Reg's good intentions, and he tries to save the situation the only way he knows how, by resigning into obedience:

> What? All right, love, all right. I leave it to you. I was only trying to help. Everybody go where Sarah tells them.[56]

Sarah starts over, patiently, like a schoolteacher with her seating chart—"Thank you. Tom. You are sitting here"—only to have Norman enter aimlessly and throw her entire arrangement off once again. This time, drained by her family's frivolous disregard, Sarah gives in to the pressures of anarchy, letting the children have their way and sit where they wish—though not without a last reprimand: "Oh , well. It's not correct."

The rest of the evening, what Annie calls their "grand reunion...with Sarah presiding," is no less disastrous, as Sarah attempts with little success to keep civil relations among the three couples—"Don't let's quarrel, please." Sarah patiently ignores Norman's insulting "small talk" and Ruth's "snide little remarks." She tries to help Tom out-jolly Norman: "Quiet," she barks to everyone, "let Tom tell his joke." And she wants to make sure Annie doesn't do all

---

[56] Alan Ayckbourn, *The Norman Conquests*, p. 67.

the work: "Reg,...offer to help." But the calm can hold for only so long, and when Reg forgets his promise and begins griping about the watery stew, Sarah breaks out her long-suffering Guardian complaint:

> It's all right for you, you don't have to cook it, do you? Think of me for a change....I mean, what rest do I get at home? Not only you to look after but the children as well.[57]

Ruth, who has been waiting for a chance at Sarah, springs into action and accuses Sarah of using her children "like some awful weapon" to establish her moral superiority. "You're always making out they're some dreadful burden," she argues, "like a penance"; and then she cruelly mimics Sarah's self-righteous attitude: "I alone who have borne children," she drones in Sarah's anguished voice, "know the true meaning of suffering."

The argument gets quickly out of hand, and in the pandemonium that follows Ruth spills Reg's wine into his lap, Sarah shrilly directs Reg not to lose his temper, Norman (shouting over the noise) blames his unfeeling, "irrational" wife Ruth for starting the fracas, and Tom (thinking Annie has been insulted) launches a blow at Norman, knocking him off his chair. Sarah tries desperately to maintain order, drumming on the table and screaming "Stop it! Stop it! Stop it!" But at the end she sits

---

[57] Alan Ayckbourn, *The Norman Conquests*, p. 73. Sarah's game here is what Eric Berne calls "Harried," with a clever touch of "Housewife's Knee" for variety (*Games People Play* [Ballantine ed., 1964], p. 102).

in what Ayckbourn describes as "*as state near to traumatic shock...visibly shaking*," and mumbling in her tears, "This is the last time I do anything for this family."

On Monday morning, after a night shuddering in bed with fury and frustration, which Reg likens to "sleeping on top of spin dryer," Sarah is up early, dressed and ready to return to her own, more orderly life. Reg wants a good breakfast, but Sarah has a sudden urge to clean her house, and wants to leave at once:

> I have to go over the house from top to bottom don't I? You may not realize it, but the house has to be cleaned. It doesn't clean itself.[58]

When feeling estranged from their families, Supervisors often seek out additional responsibilities in order to bolster their self-confidence—to prove how much they are needed—and thus, though Reg wonders innocently how the house could have gotten dirty without them in it, Sarah will not be deterred:

> It's been standing for a whole weekend. Anyway, Mrs. Bridges comes to clean tomorrow. I want to make sure it's clean before she does.[59]

However, Sarah's compulsive need to clean her nest might also have a more guilty motivation. She and Norman are in the midst of a *tête-à-tête* when Reg comes in scrounging for

---

[58] Alan Ayckbourn, *The Norman Conquests*, p. 82.
[59] Alan Ayckbourn, *The Norman Conquests*, p. 82.

food; indeed, Norman has just finished (softly, slyly) proposing to take Sarah away for an "above board" weekend holiday. "I'd book us a nice hotel," he has promised her, and then described their day:

> Breakfast in bed—separate breakfast. Separate beds. Separate rooms. Can't you imagine it? We'd wake up in the morning, side by side, in our separate rooms, and there's the sea. And we've got all day to look at it. No children to worry about. No husband to run after.[60]

Norman has been more or less flirting with Sarah all weekend, to no avail, but this time, at the end of what Sarah calls the most "shattering weekend in my life," he seems to have found his approach. Of course, Sarah is rather broken and vulnerable at the moment, but Norman's offer of a weekend of rest, free from all obligations, would be tempting to even the most undaunted Guardian. Keirsey points out that to be "passively wined, dined, and entertained. To not have to be responsible for a little while"[61] is a Guardian's ideal vacation. And though Sarah cannot quite believe she is listening to Norman's Artisan blandishments ("We'd have fun. Have you ever been to Bournemouth? It's a great place. Laugh a minute."), she heaves a far-away sigh and confesses, "I can just see us going."

But even when being seduced, a Supervisor's life is a series of duties and inconveniences, one irritating interruption

---

[60] Alan Ayckbourn, *The Norman Conquests*, p. 81.
[61] David Keirsey, *Portraits of Temperament*, p. 50.

after another, and Sarah is quickly called away from her dreamy self-indulgence. Sarah's attitude is always "If you want something doing...you might as well do it yourself," and so she gathers herself to push Reg along, to remind Tom to "take care of Annie," and to find the fuse wire so that Reg can start Ruth's car. In all the bustle of getting away, Sarah finds a private moment to invite Norman to ring her up ("I'm usually tied to the house," she whispers), although she knows full well that her self-esteem—like that of all the Guardians—lies not in adolescent sexual fantasies, but in bearing up under her burdens as a wife and mother, and in taking charge of the family:

> I've a dozen things I could be doing at home. I've got two children to worry about, a house, a husband—of sorts....I seem to be the only one in this family capable of making any sort of decision at all. I mean whether or not I like it, I seem to be the head of this family.[62]

*   *   *   *   *

Supervisors are so supremely confident in their Pygmalion projects that they often have trouble recognizing the strain their instinctive domination puts on their relationships. Torvald has no inkling of Nora's dissatisfaction until she turns on him at the end of *A Doll House*, when it is too late. And when Norman confronts Sarah with her tyranny over Reg—"what have you done to him?   Look at him in

---

[62] Alan Ayckbourn, *The Norman Conquests*, p. 182.

there...polishing plates for dear life because Sarah said so"—she brushes aside his criticism and assumes that if anything is wrong, it is with Norman. "I bet you've never washed up in your life," she scowls, and accuses him, "You don't understand me at all, do you? You don't like me and you've never tried to understand me." Indeed, of all the Guardians, Supervisors are the most difficult for the other temperaments to understand and to appreciate, whether they are Artisans like Norman, Idealists like Nora, or Rationals like Ruth. But in loving a Supervisor we need to take our cue from Reg. For all their irritating role-directiveness, Supervisors bring unflagging commitment and organization to a marriage, maintaining the house, energizing and disciplining the spouse, and as far as possible seeing to it that all members of the family obey the rules and rituals of social propriety.

Afterword

The woods are lovely, dark and deep,
But I have promises to keep,
And miles to go before I sleep,
And miles to go before I sleep.

——Robert Frost[1]

Guardians are the most conscientious and responsible of the four temperaments, sturdily anchoring our everyday world, faithfully performing the simple, familiar, and often thankless tasks to which the Artisans, Rationals, and Idealists often seem oblivious. As I have characterized them in this book, Guardians conserve and monitor the workings of family, business, and society, by protecting valuable traditions, by providing essential goods and services, by inspecting for proper compliance with the rules, and by carefully supervising the people and institutions in their charge.

---

[1] Robert Frost, "Stopping by Woods on a Snowy Evening," ll. 13-16.

The mirror of literature, as I hope my portraits in this book have shown, reflects the Guardians' industrious and meticulous behavior in amazing detail, but I must concede that, for all its accuracy, literature has great difficulty portraying the Guardians as heroically as it does the other temperaments. To most writers, Guardians are not as sensually exciting as the Artisans, not as intellectually daring as the Rationals, and not as spiritually questing as the Idealists—and thus literature rarely views them as fascinating, larger-than-life figures. To be sure, in real life Guardians are not inclined to be risk-takers, rule-breakers, or knights-errant, and though they might occasionally pause and feel the "lovely, dark and deep" call of the winter woods, as in Robert Frost's poem, they very quickly remember their promises and press on, keeping to their appointed duties. Sadly, because Guardians fulfill their responsibilities with such selfless devotion, always wanting to put others first, they bear the weight of an undeserved accusation, implicit in much of the literature, that they as a temperament are uninteresting.

Indeed, the other temperaments (in literature *and* in life, as far as I can tell) all too unfairly belittle the Guardian way of life as being dull and pedestrian. Artisans, for example, often make fun of the Guardians for being meddling and monotonous—for Sarah "racing round organizing things," or for Babbitt worrying if his secretary is "spending too much on carbon paper." Rationals at times (in their darkest moments) seem to have a more deadly ax to grind, and they

attack with a sharper irony what they regard as the
Guardians' plodding and hidebound mentality—or what
Mr. Bennet scornfully calls his wife's "weak understanding
and illiberal mind." Idealists are a bit more sympathetic
and diplomatic, though they too criticize the Guardians
quite passionately for what they believe is their arbitrary
and repressive control of the people in their lives—
"presiding," as one Idealist character describes Mrs.
Ramsay, "over destinies which she completely failed to
understand."

But surely this criticism from the other temperaments, in so
far as it is seriously intended, is unwarranted and
unnecessarily demeaning to the Guardians. In the first
place, most Guardians are far more well-rounded and mild-
tempered than these negative stereotypes suggest.
Literature tends to observe its Guardians under
extraordinary stress, when their desire for discipline is most
coercive; but in normal life, when not pushed to such
flustered extremes, Guardians go about their relationships
with good humor and a wonderful degree of social
skillfulness. And in the second place, the demands of home
life and the rigors of social organization are not, in
themselves, stifling or trivial, no matter how unimportant
they might seem to the other temperaments. Guardians
derive profound satisfaction, and significant drama, from
their memberships and their rituals, from their collections
and their codes of conduct, from their services and their
sufferings, and almost all of the authors I've selected for

this book (even those who criticize most severely) find a good deal to admire and to honor in the Guardians' struggle with life.

Very simply, Guardians make up the solid, indispensible foundation of our society—they are the cornerstones of all the institutions in our culture—and we would do well to value their rock-steady support for orderliness in our fast-paced, unstable world, an orderliness that we often carelessly take for granted. If we could all learn to respect the Guardians for their sincere concern and tireless dependability, instead of labeling them (and thus trying to change them) out of our own frustrations, then our relationships with them could be freed at least from our part in the Pygmalion project.

Appendix

The Keirsey Temperament Sorter

Please use the answer sheet on page 170.

1. **At a party do you**
   - (a) interact with many, including strangers
   - (b) interact with a few, known to you

2. **Are you more**
   - (a) realistic that speculative
   - (b) speculative than realistic

3. **Is it worse to**
   - (a) have your "head in the clouds"
   - (b) be "in a rut"

4. **Are you more impressed by**
   - (a) principles   (b) emotions

5. **Are you more drawn toward the**
   - (a) convincing   (b) touching

6. Do you prefer to work
    (a) to deadlines   (b) just "whenever"

7. Do you tend to choose
    (a) rather carefully   (b) somewhat impulsively

8. At parties do you
    (a) stay late, with increasing energy
    (b) leave early, with decreased energy

9. Are you more attracted to
    (a) what is actual   (b) what is possible

10. Are you more interested in
    (a) sensible people   (b) imaginative people

11. In judging others are you more swayed by
    (a) laws than circumstances
    (b) circumstances than laws

12. In approaching others is your inclination to be somewhat
    (a) objective   (b) personal

13. Are you more
    (a) punctual   (b) leisurely

14. Does it bother you more having things
    (a) incomplete   (b) completed

15. In your social groups do you
    (a) keep abreast of others' happenings
    (b) get behind on the news

16. In doing ordinary things are you more likely to
    (a) do it the usual way   (b) do it your own way

17. Writers should
    (a) "say what they mean and mean what they say"
    (b) express things more by use of analogy

18. **Which appeals to you more:**
    (a) consistency of thought
    (b) harmonious human relations

19. **Are you more comfortable in making**
    (a) logical judgments   (b) value judgments

20. **Do you want things**
    (a) settled and decided (b) unsettled and undecided

21. **Would you say you are more**
    (a) serious and determined (b) easy-going

22. **In phoning do you**
    (a) rarely question that it will all be said
    (b) rehearse what you'll say

23. **Facts**
    (a) "speak for themselves" (b) illustrate principles

24. **Are visionaries**
    (a) somewhat annoying   (b) rather fascinating

25. **Are you more often**
    (a) a cool-headed person   (b) a warm-hearted person

26. **Is it worse to be**
    (a) unjust   (b) merciless

27. **Should one usually let events occur**
    (a) by careful selection and choice
    (b) randomly and by chance

28. **Do you feel better about**
    (a) having purchased   (b) having the option to buy

29. **In company do you**
    (a) initiate conversation (b) wait to be approached

30. **Common sense is**
    (a) rarely questionable (b) frequently questionable

31. Children often do not
   (a) make themselves useful enough
   (b) exercise their fantasy enough

32. In making decisions do you feel more comfortable with
   (a) standards   (b) feelings

33. Are you more
   (a) firm than gentle   (b) gentle than firm

34. Which is more admirable:
   (a) the ability to organize and be methodical
   (b) the ability to adapt and make do

35. Do you put more value on the
   (a) definite   (b) open-ended

36. Does new and non-routine interaction with others
   (a) stimulate and energize you
   (b) tax your reserves

37. Are you more frequently
   (a) a practical sort of person
   (b) a fanciful sort of person

38. Are you more likely to
   (a) see how others are useful
   (b) see how others see

39. Which is more satisfying:
   (a) to discuss an issue thoroughly
   (b) to arrive at agreement on an issue

40. Which rules you more:
   (a) your head   (b) your heart

41. Are you more comfortable with work that is
   (a) contracted   (b) done on a casual basis

42. Do you tend to look for
    (a) the orderly   (b) whatever turns up

43. Do you prefer
    (a) many friends with brief contact
    (b) a few friends with more lengthy contact

44. Do you go more by
    (a) facts   (b) principles

45. Are you more interested in
    (a) production and distribution
    (b) design and research

46. Which is more of a compliment:
    (a) "There is a very logical person"
    (b) "There is a very sentimental person"

47. Do you value in yourself more that you are
    (a) unwavering   (b) devoted

48. Do you more often prefer the
    (a) final and unalterable statement
    (b) tentative and preliminary statement

49. Are you more comfortable
    (a) after a decision   (b) before a decision

50. Do you
    (a) speak easily and at length with strangers
    (b) find little to say to strangers

51. Are you more likely to trust your
    (a) experience   (b) hunch

52. Do you feel
    (a) more practical than ingenious
    (b) more ingenious than practical

53. Which person is more to be complimented: one of
    (a) clear reason   (b) strong feeling

54. Are you inclined more to be
    (a) fair-minded   (b) sympathetic

55. Is it preferable mostly to
    (a) make sure things are arranged
    (b) just let things happen

56. In relationships should most things be
    (a) renegotiable
    (b) random and circumstantial

57. When the phone rings do you
    (a) hasten to get to it first
    (b) hope someone else will answer

58. Do you prize more in yourself
    (a) a strong sense of reality (b) a vivid imagination

59. Are you drawn more to
    (a) fundamentals   (b) overtones

60. Which seems the greater error:
    (a) to be too passionate   (b) to be too objective

61. Do you see yourself as basically
    (a) hard-headed   (b) soft-hearted

62. Which situation appeals to you more:
    (a) the structured and scheduled
    (b) the unstructured and unscheduled

63. Are you a person who is more
    (a) routinized than whimsical
    (b) whimsical than routinized

64. Are you more inclined to be
    (a) easy to approach   (b) somewhat reserved

65. In writings do you prefer
    (a) the more literal   (b) the more figurative

66. Is it harder for you to
    (a) identify with others (b) utilize others

67. Which do you wish more for yourself:
    (a) clarity of reason   (b) strength of compassion

68. Which is the greater fault:
    (a) being indiscriminate (b) being critical

69. Do you prefer the
    (a) planned event   (b) unplanned event

70. Do you tend to be more
    (a) deliberate than spontaneous
    (b) spontanteous than deliberate

Answer Sheet

Enter a check for each answer in the column for **a** or **b**.

	A	B		A	B		A	B		A	B		A	B		A	B		A	B
1			2			3			4			5			6			7		
8			9			10			11			12			13			14		
15			16			17			18			19			20			21		
22			23			24			25			26			27			28		
29			30			31			32			33			34			35		
36			37			38			39			40			41			42		
43			44			45			46			47			48			49		
50			51			52			53			54			55			56		
57			58			59			60			61			62			63		
64			65			66			67			68			69			70		

1   2   3   4   3   4   5   6   5   6   7   8   7   8

1   2   3   4   5   6   7   8

E I   **S N**   **T F**   **J P**

Directions for Scoring

1. **Add down** so that the total number of "a" answers is written in the box at the bottom of each column (see next page for illustration). Do the same for the "b" answers you have checked. Each of the 14 boxes should have a number in it.

2. **Transfer the number** in box no. 1 of the answer sheet to box no. 1 below the answer sheet. Do this for box no. 2 as well. Note, however, that you have two numbers for boxes 3 through 8. Bring down the first number for each box beneath the second, as indicated by the arrows. Now add all the pairs of numbers and enter the total in the boxes below the answer sheet, so that each box has only one number (see illustration on next page).

3. **Now you have** four pairs of numbers. Circle the letter below the larger number of each pair (again, see illustration). If the two numbers of any pair are equal, then circle neither, but put a large X below them and circle it.

You have now identified your "type." It should be one of the following:

INFP	**ISFP**	**INTP**	**ISTP**
ENFP	**ESFP**	**ENTP**	**ESTP**
INFJ	**ISFJ**	**INTJ**	**ISTJ**
ENFJ	**ESFJ**	**ENTJ**	**ESTJ**

Sample Answer Sheet

See "Directions for Scoring" on the facing page.

	A	B		A	B		A	B		A	B		A	B		A	B		A	B
1	X		2	X		3	X		4		X	5		X	6	X		7		X
8	X		9	X		10	X		11		X	12		X	13	X		14	X	
15	X		16	X		17	X		18		X	19		X	20	X		21	X	
22		X	23	X		24	X		25		X	26		X	27	X		28	X	
29	X		30	X		31		X	32		X	33		X	34	X		35	X	
36	X		37	X		38	X		39		X	40		X	41	X		42	X	
43		X	44		X	45	X		46		X	47		X	48	X		49		X
50	X		51	X		52	X		53		X	54	X		55	X		56	X	
57	X		58	X		59	X		60		X	61		X	62	X		63		X
64	X		65	X		66		X	67		X	68		X	69	X		70	X	

1	8	2	2	3	9	1	4	3	8	2	4	5	0	10	6	5	1	9	6	7	10	0	8	7	7	3	8

9	1

0	10

10	0

1	8	2	2		3	11	3	4		5	1	11	6		7	11	3	8

(E) I   (S) N   T (F)   (J) P

If you have an X in your type, yours is a mixed type. An X can show up in any of the four pairs: E or I, S or N, T or F, and J or P. Hence there are 32 mixed types besides the 16 listed above:

XNTP	EXTP	ENXP	ENTX
XNTJ	EXTJ	INXP	INTX
XNFP	EXFP	ENXJ	ENFX
XNFJ	EXFJ	INXJ	INFX
XSTP	IXTP	ESXP	ESTX
XSTJ	IXTJ	ISXP	ISTX
XSFP	IXFP	ESXJ	ESFX
XSFJ	IXFJ	ISXJ	ISFX

Having identified your type, the task is now to read the type description and to decide how well or how poorly the description fits. You will find a description or portrait of your type on the page indicated in the table of contents of *Please Understand Me.* If you have an X in your type, yours is a combination of two types. If, for example, the E and I scores are equal and the type is, say XSFJ, then you would read both ESFJ and ISFJ portraits and decide for yourself which parts of each description are applicable.

Bibliography

Alexander, Franz. "The Logic of Emotions and Its Dynamic Background." *International Journal of Psychoanalysis*, 16:399-413, 1935.

_____. *Psychosomatic Medicine*. New York: W.W. Norton & Company, Inc., 1950.

Alexander, Franz, and Thomas Morton French. *Studies in Psychosomatic Medicine*. New York: The Ronald Press Company, 1948.

Allen, Walter. *The Modern Novel in Britain and the United States*. New York: E.P. Dutton & Company, Inc., 1965.

Allen, Woody. *Hannah and Her Sisters*. New York: Vintage Books, 1987.

Austen, Jane. *Pride and Prejudice*. Boston: Houghton Mifflin Company, 1956.

Ayckbourn, Alan. *The Norman Conquests*. New York: Grove Press, 1975.

Bateson, Gregory. "Toward a Theory of Schizophrenia." In *Steps To an Ecology of Mind*. New York: Ballantine Books, 1972.

Berne, Eric. *Games People Play*. New York: Ballantine Books, 1964.

Chaucer, Geoffrey. *The Canterbury Tales*. Trans. Nevill Coghill. New York: Penguin Books, 1977.

Chekov, Anton. *The Cherry Orchard*. Trans. Constance Garnett. In *Four Great Plays by Chekov*. New York: Bantam Books, 1968.

Cohen, B. Bernard. *Writing About Literature*. Glenview, Illinois: Scott, Foresman and Company, 1973.

Conrad, Joseph. *Heart of Darkness*. New York: W.W. Norton & Company, Inc., 1971.

_____. *Typhoon*. In *Joseph Conrad: Three Great Tales*. New York: Vintage Books.

Eliot, T.S. *Collected Poems, 1909-1962*. New York: Harcourt, Brace & World, Inc., 1963.

Esterson, Aaron. *Leaves of Spring*. London: Tavistock Publications, 1970.

Flaubert, Gustave. *Madame Bovary*. Trans. Francis Steegmuller. New York: The Modern Library, 1957.

Forester, C.S. *The African Queen*. Boston: Little, Brown and Company, 1968.

Forster, E.M. *Aspects of the Novel.* New York: Harcourt, Brace & World, Inc., 1954.

_____. *A Room With a View.* New York: Vintage Books.

Fowles, John. *The French Lieutenant's Woman.* New York: Signet Books, 1970.

Frazer, Sir James George. *The Golden Bough: A Study in Magic and Religion.* Abridged Edition. New York: The Macmillan Company, 1943.

Frost, Robert. *Complete Poems of Robert Frost, 1949.* New York, Chicago, and San Francisco: Holt, Rinehart and Winston, 1964.

Haley, Jay, ed. *Conversations with Milton H. Erickson, M.D., Volume I: Changing Individuals.* U.S.A.: Triangle Press, 1985.

Hamilton, Edith. *Mythology.* New York and Toronto: New American Library.

Hardy, Thomas. *Tess of the D'Urbervilles.* New York: Signet Classics, 1964.

Hesse, Hermann. *Narcissus and Goldmund.* Trans. Ursule Molinaro. New York: Farrar, Straus and Giroux, 1968.

Houghton, Walter E. *The Victorian Frame of Mind.* New Haven: Yale University Press, 1957.

Ibsen, Henrik. *A Doll House.* Trans. Rolf Fjelde. In *Ibsen: Four Major Plays.* New York: Signet Classics, 1965.

_____. *From Ibsen's Workshop.* Trans. A.G. Chater. Ed. William Archer. New York: Da Capo Press, Inc., 1978.

James, Henry. *Partial Portraits.* Ann Arbor: The University of Michigan Press, 1970.

_____. *The Bostonians.* New York: The Modern Library, 1956.

Keats, John. *Selected Poems and Letters.* Boston: Houghton Mifflin Company, 1959.

Keirsey, David. *Portraits of Temperament.* U.S.A.: Gnosology Books, Ltd., 1987.

Keirsey, David, and Marilyn Bates. *Please Understand Me: Character and Temperament Types.* U.S.A.: Gnosology Books, Ltd., 1984.

Kiley, Dan. *The Peter Pan Syndrome.* New York: Avon Books, 1983.

_____. *The Wendy Dilemma.* New York: Avon Books, 1984.

Lawrence, D.H. *Sons and Lovers.* New York: Penguin Books, 1981.

Levy, David M. *Maternal Overprotection.* New York: W.W. Norton & Company, Inc., 1966.

Lewis, Sinclair. *Babbitt.* New York: Signet Classics, 1950.

Miller, Alice. *The Drama of the Gifted Child.* Trans. Ruth Ward. New York: Basic Books, Inc., 1981.

_____. *For Your Own Good: Hidden Cruelty in Child-Rearing and the Roots of Violence.* Trans. Hildegarde and Hunter Hannum. New York: Farrar, Straus and Giroux, 1984.

_____. *Thou Shalt Not Be Aware: Society's Betrayal of the Child.* Trans. Hildegarde and Hunter Hannum. New York: New American Library, 1986.

Norwood, Robin. *Women Who Love Too Much.* New York: Pocket Books, 1986.

Ruesch, Jurgen, and Gregory Bateson. *Communication: The Social Matrix of Psychiatry.* New York: W.W. Norton & Company, Inc., 1951.

Scholes, Robert, Carl H. Klaus, and Michael Silverman. *Elements of Literature.* New York: Oxford University Press, 1978.

Shakespeare, William. *Hamlet.* Baltimore: Penguin Books, 1969.

_____. *Twelfth Night.* Baltimore: Penguin Books, 1969.

Shaw, George Bernard. *Candida.* New York: Penguin Books, 1977.

Sheridan, Richard Brinsley. *The School for Scandal.* Ed. C.J.L. Prince. London: Oxford University Press, 1971.

Tolkien, J.R.R. *The Hobbit.* New York: Ballantine Books, 1965.

Tolstoy, Leo. *The Death of Ivan Ilych and Other Stories.* Trans. Aylmer Maude. New York: Signet Classics, 1960.

Vonnegut, Kurt. *The Sirens of Titan.* New York: Delta Books, 1959.

Watzlawick, Paul, Janet Helmick Beavin, and Don D. Jackson. *Pragmatics of Human Communication.* New York: W.W. Norton & Company, Inc., 1967.

Watzlawick, Paul, John Weakland, and Richard Fisch. *Change: Principles of Problem Formation and Problem Resolution.* New York: W.W. Norton & Company, Inc., 1974.

Waugh, Evelyn. *A Handful of Dust.* Boston: Little, Brown and Company, 1962.

Wharton, Edith. *The Age of Innocence.* New York: Charles Scribner's Sons, 1948.

Wilde, Oscar. *The Importance of Being Earnest.* New York: Avon Books, 1965.

Woolf, Virginia. *To the Lighthouse.* New York: Harcourt, Brace & World, Inc., 1955.

Index

Page numbers in **boldface** reference a quotation.

Page numbers in *italics* reference a footnote.

Dr. Stephen Montgomery's *The Pygmalion Project: Love and Coercion Among the Types* is a four-volume explication of David Keirsey's views of the characteristic mating styles (and games) among the four temperaments described in Keirsey's best-seller, *Please Understand Me*. Having completed *Volume One* on the Artisan ("SP") temperament, and now *Volume Two* on the Guardian ("SJ") temperament, Montgomery is turning his attention to the two more abstract character styles, the Idealist ("NF") in *Volume Three*, and the Rational ("NT") in *Volume Four*.

Volume 3: The Idealist [in progress] will likely discuss, among other relationships, Sarah Woodruff and Charles Smithson from John Fowles's *The French Lieutenant's Woman*, Cathy and Heathcliff (and Edgar) from Emily Brontë's *Wuthering Heights*, and Tess Durbeyfield and Angel Clare from Thomas Hardy's *Tess of the D'Urbervilles*.

Volume 4: The Rational will likely discuss Elizabeth and Darcy from Jane Austen's *Pride and Prejudice*, John Galt and Dagny Taggert from Ayn Rand's *Atlas Shrugged*, and Henry Higgins and Eliza Doolittle from Bernard Shaw's *Pygmalion*.

Answer Sheet

Enter a check for each answer in the column for **a** or **b**.

	A	B		A	B		A	B		A	B		A	B		A	B		A	B
1			2			3			4			5			6			7		
8			9			10			11			12			13			14		
15			16			17			18			19			20			21		
22			23			24			25			26			27			28		
29			30			31			32			33			34			35		
36			37			38			39			40			41			42		
43			44			45			46			47			48			49		
50			51			52			53			54			55			56		
57			58			59			60			61			62			63		
64			65			66			67			68			69			70		

1   2   3   4   3   4   5   6   5   6   7   8   7   8

1 [ ] 2   3 [ ] 4   5 [ ] 6   7 [ ] 8

E I   **S N**   **T F**   **J P**

Answer Sheet

Enter a check for each answer in the column for **a** or **b**.

	A	B		A	B		A	B		A	B		A	B		A	B		A	B
1			2			3			4			5			6			7		
8			9			10			11			12			13			14		
15			16			17			18			19			20			21		
22			23			24			25			26			27			28		
29			30			31			32			33			34			35		
36			37			38			39			40			41			42		
43			44			45			46			47			48			49		
50			51			52			53			54			55			56		
57			58			59			60			61			62			63		
64			65			66			67			68			69			70		

1   2   3   4   3   4   5   6   5   6   7   8   7   8

1   2   3   4   5   6   7   8

E I   **S N**   **T F**   **J P**

Answer Sheet

Enter a check for each answer in the column for **a** or **b**.

	A	B		A	B		A	B		A	B		A	B		A	B		A	B
1			2			3			4			5			6			7		
8			9			10			11			12			13			14		
15			16			17			18			19			20			21		
22			23			24			25			26			27			28		
29			30			31			32			33			34			35		
36			37			38			39			40			41			42		
43			44			45			46			47			48			49		
50			51			52			53			54			55			56		
57			58			59			60			61			62			63		
64			65			66			67			68			69			70		

1   2   3   4   3   4   5   6   5   6   7   8   7   8

1   2

E I

3   4

S N

5   6

T F

7   8

J P

Answer Sheet

Enter a check for each answer in the column for **a** or **b**.

	A	B		A	B		A	B		A	B		A	B		A	B		A	B
1			2			3			4			5			6			7		
8			9			10			11			12			13			14		
15			16			17			18			19			20			21		
22			23			24			25			26			27			28		
29			30			31			32			33			34			35		
36			37			38			39			40			41			42		
43			44			45			46			47			48			49		
50			51			52			53			54			55			56		
57			58			59			60			61			62			63		
64			65			66			67			68			69			70		

1   2   3   4   3   4   5   6   5   6   7   8   7   8

1   2   3   4   5   6   7   8

E I   **S N**   **T F**   **J P**

Answer Sheet

Enter a check for each answer in the column for **a** or **b**.

	A	B		A	B		A	B		A	B		A	B		A	B		A	B
1			2			3			4			5			6			7		
8			9			10			11			12			13			14		
15			16			17			18			19			20			21		
22			23			24			25			26			27			28		
29			30			31			32			33			34			35		
36			37			38			39			40			41			42		
43			44			45			46			47			48			49		
50			51			52			53			54			55			56		
57			58			59			60			61			62			63		
64			65			66			67			68			69			70		

1 [ ] 2   3 [ ] 4   3 [ ] 4   5 [ ] 6   5 [ ] 6   7 [ ] 8   7 [ ] 8

1 [ ] 2   3 [ ] 4   5 [ ] 6   7 [ ] 8

E I　　　**S N**　　　**T F**　　　**J P**

Answer Sheet

Enter a check for each answer in the column for **a** or **b**.

	A	B		A	B		A	B		A	B		A	B		A	B		A	B
1			2			3			4			5			6			7		
8			9			10			11			12			13			14		
15			16			17			18			19			20			21		
22			23			24			25			26			27			28		
29			30			31			32			33			34			35		
36			37			38			39			40			41			42		
43			44			45			46			47			48			49		
50			51			52			53			54			55			56		
57			58			59			60			61			62			63		
64			65			66			67			68			69			70		

1   2   3   4   3   4   5   6   5   6   7   8   7   8

1   2   3   4   5   6   7   8

E I   **S N**   **T F**   **J P**

Answer Sheet

Enter a check for each answer in the column for **a** or **b**.

	A	B		A	B		A	B		A	B		A	B		A	B		A	B
1			2			3			4			5			6			7		
8			9			10			11			12			13			14		
15			16			17			18			19			20			21		
22			23			24			25			26			27			28		
29			30			31			32			33			34			35		
36			37			38			39			40			41			42		
43			44			45			46			47			48			49		
50			51			52			53			54			55			56		
57			58			59			60			61			62			63		
64			65			66			67			68			69			70		

1   2 3   4 3   4 5   6 5   6 7   8 7   8

1   2   3   4   5   6   7   8

E I   **S N**   **T F**   **J P**

Answer Sheet

Enter a check for each answer in the column for **a** or **b**.

	A	B		A	B		A	B		A	B		A	B		A	B		A	B
1			2			3			4			5			6			7		
8			9			10			11			12			13			14		
15			16			17			18			19			20			21		
22			23			24			25			26			27			28		
29			30			31			32			33			34			35		
36			37			38			39			40			41			42		
43			44			45			46			47			48			49		
50			51			52			53			54			55			56		
57			58			59			60			61			62			63		
64			65			66			67			68			69			70		

1   2 3   4 3   4 5   6 5   6 7   8 7   8

1   2   3   4   5   6   7   8

E I   **S N**   **T F**   **J P**

PORTRAITS OF TEMPERAMENT

Portraits of Temperament is David Keirsey's most recent thinking on the ingrained attitudes and habitual actions of the four basic personality types, which he now renames the Artisans, Guardians, Rationals, and Idealists. Keirsey summarizes the four temperaments, showing how the behavior of each is either concrete or abstract, cooperative or pragmatic, directive or informative, and finally, assertive or responsive. The book includes two brief self-scoring personality tests to assist in observing the differences and similarities among us.

Published by
Prometheus Nemesis Book Company

LOVE, COERCION, AND THE ARTISAN

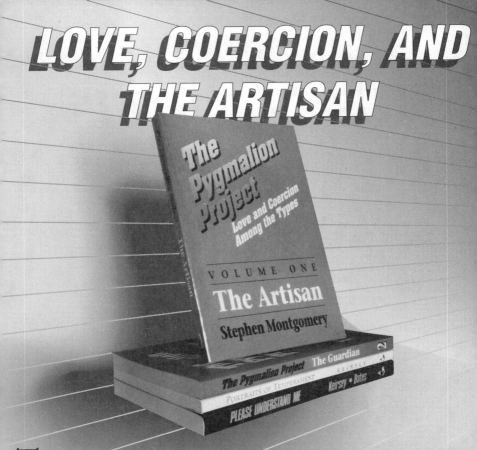

The Pygmalion Project: Volume I, The Artisan, by Dr. Stephen Montgomery (the editor of *Please Understand Me*) investigates the styles of love and coercion among the Keirseyan temperaments, taking famous characters from literature and film as provocative case studies. *Volume I, The Artisan* approaches the art of loving from the Artisans' point-of-view, by examining their playful and charming way in relationships with Guardian ("SJ"), Rational ("NT"), and Idealist ("NF") partners. Begin by completing Keirsey's new personality test, and then read about the Artisan mating game, how they delight and dismay their loved ones, as presented in the pages of D. H. Lawrence, Ernest Hemingway, F. Scott Fitzgerald, and eight other authors. More importantly learn more about Keirsey's concept of the Pygmalion Project—how we try to sculpt our loved ones into copies of ourselves, and how we are manipulated by them in return. If you've ever been in love with an Artisan (or ever been fooled by one), *The Pygmalion Project* will prove fascinating reading.

Published by
Prometheus Nemesis Book Company

THE GUARDIAN'S PYGMALION PROJECT

The second part of Dr. Stephen Montgomery's quartet on love and coercion among the types focuses on the Guardians' ("SJ") uniquely responsible style of caring for others. Montgomery (the editor of *Please Understand Me*) has selected characters from works of Jane Austen, Sinclair Lewis, Virginia Woolf, and half a dozen other authors, to bring to life the Guardian's parental way in love and marriage, and to illustrate their earnest style of interpersonal manipulation—what Keirsey calls the Pygmalion Project. The book examines the Guardians both as instigators and as victims of marital games with the Rationals ("NTs"), the Idealists ("NFs"), and particularly with the childlike Artisans ("SPs"). If you have a Guardian spouse (or even a Guardian parent), *The Pygmalion Project: Volume 2, The Guardian* will help you understand and appreciate them.

Published by
Prometheus Nemesis Book Company

ORDER FORM

	UNIT PRICE	QUANTITY ORDERED	TOTAL PRICE
Please Understand Me Keirsey, Bates	11.95		
National Bestseller. Nearly one million copies sold. A 25 year clinical study of differences in temperament and character in mating, parenting, teaching, and leading. Includes a personality test to identify type.			
Portraits of Temperament Keirsey	9.95		
Artisan, Guardian, Rational, and Idealist personalities are described in terms of how concrete or abstract, cooperative or pragmatic, directive or informative, and assertive or responsive the different types are. Includes two personality tests to identify type.			
The Pygmalion Project: *Love and Coercion Among the Types*			
Volume 1, The Artisan Montgomery	9.95		
Volumn 1 looks at love and coercion between Artisan types ["SP"] and Guardian ["SJ"], Rational ["NT"], and Idealist ["NF"] types, as described in the pages of D.H. Lawrence, Hemingway, Fitzgerald, and several others.			
Volume 2, The Guardian Montgomery	9.95		
Volume 2 looks at love and coercion among the types from the Guardian ["SJ"] point-of-view, with examples from Evelyn Waugh, Jane Austen, Sinclair Lewis, and several others.			
The Keirsey Temperament Sorter	.25		
A brief self-scoring test of personality type from *Please Understand Me* to supplement observation.			

S H I P P I N G

Order Subtotal		USA	Outside USA
0 – $ 49.99		$ 2.00	$ 3.50
$ 50.00 – $ 99.99		$ 3.00	$ 6.00
$ 100.00 – $ 149.99		$ 3.50	$ 8.50
$ 150.00 – $ 199.99		$ 4.00	$ 10.50

SUBTOTAL [   ]

6% SALES TAX (Calif. only) [   ]

SHIPPING [   ]

TOTAL ENCLOSED [   ]

NAME _____

STREET OR BOX NUMBER _____

CITY _____ STATE _____ ZIP _____

CALL (619) 632-1575   FAX (619) 944-0845

For UPS shipping charges (delivery in less than 4-6 weeks), or for ordering related publications, discs, audiotapes, or videotapes.

Please enclose this order form in an envelope with your check (in U.S. Dollars only) and mail it to:

Prometheus Nemesis Book Company
Post Office Box 2748 • Del Mar, CA 92014

ORDER FORM

	UNIT PRICE	QUANTITY ORDERED	TOTAL PRICE

Please Understand Me Keirsey, Bates _____ — 11.95

National Bestseller. Nearly one million copies sold.
A 25 year clinical study of differences in temperament and character in mating, parenting, teaching, and leading. Includes a personality test to identify type.

Portraits of Temperament Keirsey _____ — 9.95

Artisan, Guardian, Rational, and Idealist personalities are described in terms of how concrete or abstract, cooperative or pragmatic, directive or informative, and assertive or responsive the different types are. Includes two personality tests to identify type.

The Pygmalion Project:
Love and Coercion Among the Types

Volume 1, The Artisan Montgomery _____ — 9.95

Volumn 1 looks at love and coercion between Artisan types ["SP"] and Guardian ["SJ"], Rational ["NT"], and Idealist ["NF"] types, as described in the pages of D.H. Lawrence, Hemingway, Fitzgerald, and several others.

Volume 2, The Guardian Montgomery _____ — 9.95

Volume 2 looks at love and coercion among the types from the Guardian ["SJ"] point-of-view, with examples from Evelyn Waugh, Jane Austen, Sinclair Lewis, and several others.

The Keirsey Temperament Sorter _____ — .25

A brief self-scoring test of personality type from *Please Understand Me* to supplement observation.

S H I P P I N G

Order Subtotal		USA	Outside USA
0 – $ 49.99		$ 2.00	$ 3.50
$ 50.00 – $ 99.99		$ 3.00	$ 6.00
$ 100.00 – $ 149.99		$ 3.50	$ 8.50
$ 150.00 – $ 199.99		$ 4.00	$ 10.50

SUBTOTAL [ ]

6% SALES TAX (Calif. only) [ ]

SHIPPING [ ]

TOTAL ENCLOSED [ ]

NAME _____

STREET OR BOX NUMBER _____

CITY _____ STATE _____ ZIP _____

CALL (619) 632-1575   FAX (619) 944-0845

For UPS shipping charges (delivery in less than 4-6 weeks), or for ordering related publications, discs, audiotapes, or videotapes.

 Please enclose this order form in an envelope with your check (in U.S. Dollars only) and mail it to:

Prometheus Nemesis Book Company
Post Office Box 2748 • Del Mar, CA 92014